Marketing Workbook
for Nonprofit Organizations

Gary J. Stern

Amherst H. Wilder Foundation
St. Paul, Minnesota

We thank the David and Lucile Packard Foundation, Los
California, for underwriting development of this book.

This workbook was developed by the Services to Organizations' Community Services Group (formerly Management Support Services), a program of the Amherst H. Wilder Foundation in Saint Paul, Minnesota. The Community Services Group works in the Saint Paul-Minneapolis metropolitan area to strengthen the capacity of individuals, organizations, and other groups to improve their communities.

Community Services Group consultants are available nationally to present training workshops and keynote presentations on marketing, strategic planning, service effectiveness and other topics related to nonprofit organizations.

The Amherst H. Wilder Foundation is one of the largest and oldest endowed human service agencies in America. For more than eighty years, the Wilder Foundation has provided human services responsive to the welfare needs of the community, all without regard to or discrimination on account of nationality, sex, color, religious scruples, or prejudices.

We hope you find this workbook helpful! Should you need additional information about our services, please contact: Community Services Group, Amherst H. Wilder Foundation, 919 Lafond Avenue, Saint Paul, MN 55104, phone (612) 642-4022.

Other books available from the Wilder Foundation: ***Strategic Planning Workbook for Nonprofit Organizations; Collaboration: What Makes It Work;*** and ***Collaboration Handbook: Creating, Sustaining, and Enjoying the Journey.*** See last page for details and ordering information. For further information, please contact: Publishing Center, Amherst H. Wilder Foundation, 919 Lafond Avenue, Saint Paul, MN 55104, 1-800-274-6024.

Written by Gary J. Stern
Designed by Rebecca Andrews
Illustrated by Giora Carmi
Edited by Bryan Barry and Carol Lukas
Copy Edited by Menia Buckner and Deborah Vajda

This book is dedicated to my father, Lester A. Stern, a wonderful man and marketer par excellence.

Special thanks to Emil Angelica, Scot Covey, Gayle Cupit, Claudia Dengler, Sandra Larson, Ellen Sue Stern, and Michael Winer.

Manufactured in the United States of America

Fourth printing, 1994

Library of Congress Catalog Card Number: 90-83183

ISBN 0-940-06901-6

Contents

Appendices

Exchanging something of value for something you need

PART
I

Demystifying Marketing

THERE'S A SPIRIT TO IT

Effective marketing makes things happen—funding increases, an empty hall fills with people, the phone rings like crazy, human needs are more powerfully met. There's a spirit to it that says "Anything is possible!" and inspires a *marketing mind* that is always on the lookout for ways to bring a vision into reality.

In some marketing meetings, the air is electric. Ideas come fast, connections happen, people see something come to life. It's like that old Judy Garland and Mickey Rooney movie where one of the kids says, "Let's do a show!" and another pipes up, "My uncle has a barn!" then another, "I know where we can get some old costumes!" And in the next scene, swarms of kids, and carpenters, and the mayor and police chief are all dashing about helping put up the show. Which ends up on Broadway.

(It's not often so simple, of course, but that's the idea.)

Marketing is a new world for many nonprofits. This workbook is meant to welcome you to that world in a friendly and informative way. Marketing can help you:

▲ Define your unique niche and be sure you have the right services to meet people's needs.
▲ Reach the audiences you want with a message that motivates people to respond.
▲ Decide what you want, go after it, and become a more prosperous organization with increased resources to carry out your mission.
▲ Stand out from the crowd and attract the kind of attention, support, and enthusiasm you need and deserve.
▲ Have a greater impact on the social welfare agenda in your community and beyond.

Marketing doesn't have to be confusing and complex. This workbook provides basic steps that any organization can learn and use. Once you've got it down, you will have a valuable tool, and perhaps a new perspective, that will prove beneficial time and again.

But some nonprofits are skeptical. Isn't marketing just for selling consumer products? Herbert Chao Gunther is director of San Francisco's nationally acclaimed Public Media Center. He responds to this skepticism, saying,

> The reason I resist being called an advertising man is obviously that advertising is perceived as the whisper in the ear that tells you you're bad, you're wrong, you're different unless you buy something. Folks who are working for social change need to learn to use the media to turn that message around and change the whisper to something like, "If you do this kind of work, you're good, you're right." [1]

Marketing is not hucksterism. It is not devious manipulation. It is not high-pressure selling. And it need not in any way compromise your ethics, your services, your cause, or your budget.

Effective marketing makes things happen—funding increases, an empty hall fills with people, the phone rings like crazy, human needs are more powerfully met.

---

[1] Herbert Chao Gunther, "The 1987 Esquire Register", **Esquire** (December 1987), p. 104.

In this book, you will learn about marketing as a creative enterprise undertaken with a caring spirit. Marketing is necessary to help nonprofits promote their values, accomplish their missions, and develop increased resources to address a range of compelling concerns. In every respect, your marketing effort can reflect the heart and soul of your work. When you are successful in your aims, the results will enliven and enrich both your organization and those you serve.

▲

MARKETING IS ALL ABOUT EXCHANGES

Here is a basic definition of marketing for nonprofits:

Marketing is a process that helps you exchange something of value for something you need.

We all take part in *exchanges* and are most familiar with the kind we make at the store, when we pay 99¢ for a loaf of bread. We give something of value to the grocer—money—in exchange for something we need—food. We have an exchange relationship with the storekeeper that is *mutually satisfying*. We each get our needs met and we both think it's a fair deal.

Marketing helps set up exchange relationships, and in the nonprofit world there is quite a range of them. Nonprofits make exchanges with their program participants or audience, with funders, volunteers, referral sources, friends, elected officials, the media, other nonprofits, businesses and corporations—the list goes on and on. In every successful exchange, the nonprofit offers something of value to others and receives something it needs in return. The diagram on the next page illustrates this idea.

The examples in the diagram are mutually satisfying exchanges because both parties benefit; they each get something they value. However, exchanges like this don't happen—except by coincidence—unless someone takes the initiative.

When *you* have something of value and want to exchange it for something you need, it's *up to you* to initiate, cultivate, and nurture exchange relationships. In other words, it's time to get into marketing.

▲

Examples of three nonprofit exchanges.

1. *A mental health clinic wants county caseworkers to make referrals to its new intervention service for multiproblem families.*

Mental Health Clinic **The Exchange** **County**

Effective services →

← Referrals & fees

▲ Offers services that improve family functioning
▲ Needs referrals
▲ Needs revenue

▲ Values services that improve family functioning
▲ Has families appropriate for service
▲ Has funds

2. *A neighborhood improvement association wants volunteers from an area corporation for a community paint-a-thon.*

Neighborhood Association **The Exchange** **Corporation**

Good community relations →

← Volunteers

▲ Offers excellent community relations opportunity
▲ Offers attractive volunteer opportunity
▲ Needs volunteers

▲ Values good community relations

▲ Has ability to recruit volunteers

3. *An AIDS project wants a school board to approve introduction of its prevention curriculum.*

AIDS Project **The Exchange** **School Board**

Greater student awareness →

← Permission & cooperation

▲ Offers proven, sensitive approach

▲ Needs approval

▲ Values students' safety

▲ Has authority to approve curriculum

THE MARKETING PROCESS

This book introduces five marketing steps. Succeeding chapters provide guidance, suggestions, and tips for each part of the process.

The Steps are:

STEP 1—Set marketing goals

STEP 2—Position your organization

STEP 3—Conduct a marketing audit

STEP 4—Develop a marketing plan

STEP 5—Develop a promotion campaign

In smaller nonprofits, marketing steps can usually be completed for the organization as a whole. Larger multiservice groups generally look at marketing for the overall organization and at the division or program level. In this type of situation, it is important that plans be developed by those most responsible for carrying them out *and* that everyone work hard to identify common goals and coordinate efforts to meet them.

STEP 1 Set marketing goals

Setting goals is the first step because goals provide direction for your total marketing effort. It is important early on to be as clear as possible about what you want to accomplish. Your goals tell you what success will look like and help you focus your attention in order to achieve it.

There are two kinds of marketing goals, *action goals* and *image goals*.

Set marketing goals

1. **Action goals.** *You want marketing to produce specific, measurable results for your organization.* Action goals relate to things you can count: the number of people who attend an event or sign up for a program; the amount of money raised or new members gained from the annual campaign.

   Sample action goals: *The clean-water group wants a 15-percent increase in membership during the coming year.*

   The adoption agency wants to attract eight participants for a monthly teen-mom support group.

2. **Image goals.** *You want to be better known or in some way change how you are seen.* If you are just starting up, adding a new program, suffering from an outdated image, or evolving significantly as an organization, you will want to set *image goals*.

Sample image goals: *A clean-water group wants to be seen as a leading regional advocate on environmental affairs.*

An adoption agency wants to update its image to reflect a broader range of family services.

The goals you set should strike a balance between what you ideally want to accomplish and what is possible. It's important to set your sights high *and* to respect down-to-earth limitations of time, resources, and outside factors beyond your control. The bottom line on marketing goals is furthering the organization's mission. Whether you're out to attract people, attract attention, raise funds, or raise a fuss, it's all done—and done only—if it serves to advance the cause.

Knowing what you want provides direction for your marketing effort—and for use of this book. You may have action goals, image goals, or both. *It is necessary to work through only the marketing steps that will help you reach your particular goals.* The goals you set may feel somewhat tentative at this early stage. As you learn more through subsequent steps, it is perfectly okay to revise them.

STEP 2   Position your organization

If you are unclear about what your image should be—how you want to be seen by others—then completing Step 2 is important to your marketing effort. Positioning means finding and establishing your *niche* or unique role in the community. It helps you define your character and *how you want to be seen.*

Positioning responds to "big picture" questions about your organization or program and gives you a statement of reputation to be reinforced throughout your marketing effort. As your niche becomes well known, your name will be firmly associated with the unique contribution you make ("Oh, they're the people who _____"). When people can identify your niche, they know what you offer them as well as what *they* might offer *you.* You become easily approachable by *others* seeking exchange relationships.

Position your organization

Working through positioning is critical if you're the new kid on the block, but can be equally important to established groups. If you are seen as "out of step with the times" or if people can't recognize how you might meet their needs, then positioning may be key to your future success.

The positioning process in this book will help you clarify what needs you address in the community and the distinctive impact you want to make. You will develop a concise positioning statement. Then you can go on to gain the kind of recognition you want.

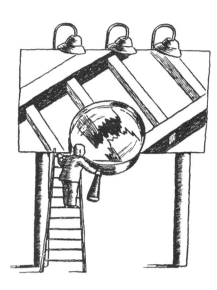

Conduct a marketing audit

STEP 3   Conduct a marketing audit

In the first two steps you decide what you want and how you want to be seen.

In Step 3, you take stock of your current marketing efforts and decide what you might change, add, or improve in order to achieve your goals.

A marketing audit is simply a short series of questions you answer to get an overall picture of where you stand right now in regard to marketing. You conduct an audit using the *"Six Ps of Marketing."** The *Six Ps* provide the central framework we will use to understand marketing issues, diagnose problems, and develop marketing plans. With these six words as checkpoints, you will find that marketing isn't mysterious at all.

The *Six Ps* are:

1. **PRODUCT**—what you offer
2. **PUBLICS**—those with whom you want to make exchanges
3. **PRICE**—how much you charge
4. **PLACE**—where the product is available
5. **PRODUCTION**—how well you can meet demand
6. **PROMOTION**—what you do to motivate people to respond

The questions for the marketing audit are based on the *Six Ps*. Working through the questions might take as little as a few minutes at your desk or can involve extensive research and a good amount of time. When you have finished, you will know what additional information you need to make sound marketing decisions, what adjustments are necessary to solve problems, and if you need to change or expand your promotional efforts. It's like going to the eye doctor to have your prescription checked. You find out how good your eyesight is and what corrections are needed to give you better vision.

---

* You may have seen other lists of the Ps of Marketing. And you may have noticed that no two authors or instructors seem to use exactly the same words. This group of Ps is geared to the specific concerns of nonprofit organizations.

STEP 4 Develop a marketing plan

Once you've done your audit, you will know where your strengths and weaknesses are regarding marketing and what needs to be changed. With that information, you can develop a marketing plan that lays out how the *Six Ps* need to be aligned in order to achieve your marketing goals. Then you can decide on the steps necessary to implement the plan, who's going to do what, by when, and with what resources and support.

When most people say "We need a marketing plan" they usually mean they want a *promotion* plan. That's because marketing as a whole is often confused with promotion—which is important—but comes at the tail end of the process. Getting the first five *Ps* lined up comes first. That means you take steps such as market research to get any additional information you need and make internal changes to remove roadblocks to the exchanges you want. If something is left out of whack with any of the *Ps*, it can throw your effort off kilter down the line.

Develop a marketing plan

Having your *Ps* in line looks like this:

Product	*You have a high-quality program, service, or product that meets people's needs.*
Publics	*You know with whom you're going to exchange the product and its benefits to them.*
Price	*The price is right—not too high, not too low.*
Place	*The product is accessible.*
Production	*You can effectively meet demand.*
Promotion	*You use strong techniques that motivate people to respond.*

Not every marketing plan calls for promotion. Sometimes marketing goals can be achieved through internal changes alone—adding new program elements, changing your price, improving customer service, or other such adjustments to bring the first five *Ps* into line.

Develop a promotion campaign

STEP 5   Develop a promotion campaign

The majority of marketing plans *do* call for a promotion campaign. They range from modest—a flyer and notice in the church bulletin—to extravagant—four-color posters, TV commercials, and special events featuring casts of thousands.

Whether small-scale or large, promotion campaigns include all the ways you communicate in order to create an image and motivate people to respond. Promotion is oriented to the *outside* world. You purposefully and deliberately call attention to yourself—often the more the better. Through promotion, you open up your doors and invite people in.

An effective promotion campaign helps to create or reinforce the *image* you want for your organization and conveys a specific *message* that tells people what you want them to do. *(Recycle! Call for more information! Don't share needles.)* A campaign employs a mix of promotional *techniques,* each chosen for its individual usefulness as well as how it fits together with the others. Twenty-seven techniques are introduced and explained later in this book.

When you have completed development of your promotion campaign, you will know:

▲ What techniques you plan to use.
▲ How things will look and what they will say.
▲ Who will implement the campaign (including outside vendors), by when, and at what cost.

Many people particularly enjoy this marketing step. You often have wonderful materials to show off, and putting any aspect of the campaign into action is, in itself, a visible accomplishment.

Marketing, strategic planning, and program development

People frequently ask how marketing fits with other organizational efforts such as strategic planning and program development. Here is the answer.

Strategic planning charts the overall direction for an organization and names the major steps it will take to achieve its goals. The call for marketing is often an *outgrowth* of strategic planning—the need for more or better exchange relationships is recognized and addressed as a part of the plan. Some groups successfully go into marketing without a strategic plan in place, but if larger organizational concerns continually crop up, it is best to suspend marketing planning and deal with strategic issues first.

Many groups new to marketing make a common mistake when it comes to program development. Something is created and then people turn to marketing to "sell it."

Instead, look at marketing as an integral part of your program planning and development efforts.

Nonprofits that have adopted this approach will testify to savings of time and money, faster community recognition for their efforts, and better program results.

Successful marketing is a sustained effort

Your marketing plan and promotion campaign will produce great results only if they are well executed. It is important to regularly evaluate your progress and be flexible and responsive. Follow-through is paramount. As you go along, you will gain new insights, opportunity may knock, or you may run into unexpected problems. If the marketing plan you labored over turns out to be flawed, go ahead and change it. If your intuition tells you to try a new promotional technique, see if you can work it in.

The focus at all times is achieving your marketing goals. To help boost your implementation efforts, lists of tips and rules of thumb are provided throughout the book.

Marketing success comes from solid exchange relationships. Like all healthy relationships, these develop over time and require ongoing care and attention. One of the biggest mistakes people make in marketing is thinking it's a one-shot deal. Good marketing is the exact opposite. It is a sustained effort.

The word to remember is persistence. Here, nonprofits can take a valuable lesson from the for-profit world. The marketing giants continually analyze product quality and know their promotional messages must be repeated often for customers to really take them in. Nonprofit organizations must also sustain their marketing efforts in order to realize success.

Right now, just starting with marketing, you might feel a bit like a stranger in a strange land. Keeping up with marketing will be much simpler after you have completed and evaluated an initial effort. You will have a better sense of "what works," be more easily able to identify and correct problems, and be prepared to respond more quickly to opportunities that arise. Many groups go on to routinely develop annual marketing plans.

Marketing becomes a powerful tool when you master its use. In the best of times it is a means of furthering growth. In the worst of times it can mean survival. At all times good marketing is like planting trees: with tending and time there is fruit.

▲

Marketing becomes a powerful tool when you master its use. In the best of times it is a means of furthering growth. In the worst of times it can mean survival. At all times good marketing is like planting trees: with tending and time there is fruit.

How to Use This Book

The *Marketing Workbook* is designed to help you identify and meet *your particular needs.* You can use the book to:

The workbook format is flexible. If you want to bite off only a small piece at a time, pick and choose the sections that are relevant.

▲ Increase your overall understanding of marketing and how it can help you accomplish your mission.
▲ Develop and implement an organization-wide marketing plan.
▲ Develop and implement marketing plans for individual programs, services, or products.
▲ Diagnose and solve marketing problems.
▲ Plan and implement targeted promotion campaigns.
▲ Gain an exciting new outlook.

The workbook format is flexible. If your marketing challenge requires a comprehensive approach, this book offers it. If you want to bite off only a small piece at a time, pick and choose the sections that are relevant. If changing the order of the steps makes better sense to you, feel free to do so.

To help you decide what is important for you to consider, the beginning of each step is flagged with this sign:

You are in the right place in this book if:

It will certainly be helpful to read through the whole book and become better acquainted with all the steps, but use the "right place" signs to decide where you want to dig in and spend your time right now.

There are worksheets for each of the five marketing steps. Completed samples are included at the end of each step. Blank worksheets are in **Appendix F**. Please feel free to make as many copies as you like, and save the originals for future use.

To get the most out of this book...

1. Adapt the workbook to your own style.

Every nonprofit has its own way of making decisions and getting things done most effectively. You can complete any or all of the marketing steps in committee, by department, with the board, or alone at your desk. Adapt the workbook to your culture and style.

2. Involve the right people.

It is important that board members, staff, and volunteers understand and feel a part of your marketing efforts. Be sure to *inform* everyone and follow this guide for involvement:

▲ People in leadership positions should, *at minimum,* be involved in decisions related to goals and positioning.
▲ People in management and staff positions should, *at minimum,* be involved in decisions that affect day-to-day operations.

If you are putting together a marketing task force or committee, invite representatives of your participant or customer groups to contribute. The "consumer" perspective is invaluable.

3. Keep the process alive.

Responsiveness and flexibility are crucial to success in marketing, so it is important to be open to adapting your plans. Come back to the book as often as necessary to refresh your understanding, complete sections that may not have applied earlier, and review the many tips for implementation.

4. Follow through!

Make sure you have the organizational commitment and resources to follow through on your decisions about marketing. Very little is more discouraging than making earnest plans that do not lead to action.

As you get started, let this couplet by Goethe inspire you:

> *Whatever you can do, or dream you can...begin it.*
> *Boldness has genius, power and magic in it.*

▲▲

PART

Your Marketing Effort

Setting goals is Step 1 of the marketing process because goals provide direction for your overall effort. It is important early on to be as clear as possible about what you want to accomplish. Your goals tell you what success will look like and help focus your attention in order to achieve it.

This chapter guides you through setting two types of marketing goals. As a part of the process, you will imagine the ideal for your organization and think through the resources and time you can realistically commit to marketing.

Step 1

Set Marketing Goals

You are in the right place in this book if:

☐ You are just about to "get into" marketing.

☐ You want to be clear about the purpose and direction of your marketing effort.

☐ You want to be specific about the results you are aiming for.

Set marketing goals

SET MARKETING GOALS

Setting your sights

Marketing goals clarify what you want to achieve through marketing and how you will define success. This is the first step in marketing because it provides a compass for your overall effort. With that compass you continually orient your efforts in the right direction to benefit your organization.

There are two categories of marketing goals:

▲ **Action goals.** *You want marketing to produce specific, measurable results for your organization.*
▲ **Image goals.** *You want to be better known or in some way change how you are seen.*

Your marketing effort may focus most strongly on action goals, on image goals, or give equal weight to both. Your goals can cover any period of time. They may target the number of people you want at an open house next month, the reputation you want for your organization next year, or changes in community attitudes you want in the next decade. As you go on with marketing, your goals may change. It's fine to start with your best estimates and make adjustments later.

Goal-setting Worksheet

There is one worksheet for setting marketing goals, **Worksheet 1.** A completed sample can be found on page 23 (blank copy on page 109).

Setting action goals

Action goals are concrete. They target the specific, measurable results you want for your organization and by when. They usually have to do with numbers—how many tickets, how many participants, how much money, how many members, and so on.

Sometimes your action goals are determined, at least in part, by others. When you receive a grant or win a contract there are usually target numbers you are committed to produce.

Marketing goals clarify what you want to achieve through marketing and how you will define success.

Here is an example of an organization's action goals:

A dynamic Project with Industry (PWI) in a mid-sized metropolitan area has worked for 10 years to increase employment opportunities for its participants: people with disabilities. The agency is federally funded and makes 250 job placements per year. PWI has an Advisory Board made up of area business leaders and an Employment Committee of nearly 150 employers who have hired people with disabilities or expressed an interest in doing so. Employment Committee members regularly alert PWI to job openings and often consider candidates referred by the agency.

PWI's most critical action goal is set for it. The federal contract calls for 250 job placements each year. Performance on this goal has been good, with some ups and downs over the past three years. Staff is concerned, however, that the trend toward higher-qualified candidates doesn't match up to the level of interest from employers. At present, the number of job placements is acceptable, but staff is looking to the future.

The majority of interest in job candidates comes through employers who belong to the PWI Employment Committee. The only requirement for membership is a commitment from employers to consider people with disabilities as candidates for available po-

sitions. The committee grew rapidly at the beginning of the project but has leveled off in recent years, with two or three new members basically replacing those who drop out.

Staff asks the Advisory Board if they believe they have peers in their industries who might be interested in joining the Employment Committee if approached. Board members are sure there are many who would join and offer to suggest lists of "prospects." Staff is excited at the possibility of adding new members with an up-front understanding of PWI's ability to provide candidates for upper-level jobs.

To keep meeting its placement goals, PWI needs to increase interest in candidates with upper-level skills.

The action goals:

1. *Continue placing 250 people with disabilities in jobs each year.*

2. *Increase job postings for upper-level positions from current Employment Committee members from an average of 2 per month to 10 per month.*

3. *Add 20 new employers to the Employment Committee within one year.*

Your action goals may be very broad and cover a number of years or be tightly focused, with the expectation of faster results. You may have many goals or only one. Each situation is unique, and your goals should correspond to what your organization needs.

You will answer four questions to set your action goals.

1. What are the absolute best results you could hope for? By when?

It's important to start here, setting your sights high. If you have to make compromises it is best to make them with the ideal, not with goals already watered down by today's realities. Sometimes naming the ideal outcome is just the touch of boldness that launches you on a course that brings it to your door.

2. What outside factors might help or hinder your ability to achieve this ideal?

Outside factors are anything in the marketplace that affect you—things like prevailing attitudes, the economy, trends, legislation, population, and competition. If you are considering a highly involved or risky venture, you might need a detailed feasibility study, but if not, you simply need to bring enough knowledge to bear so you know what challenges you face. It is important to look at what seems to be in your favor, too.

Set your sights high

One factor you should definitely consider is the size of your market and how big a share your goals represent. (The PWI going after twenty employers with particular hiring needs in a big metropolitan area is one thing. Getting twenty from a small town would be another.)

3. How will realities of budget, staff/volunteer time, and other capabilities affect your effort to achieve these results?

What can you handle? Do you have enough time and resources to make sure your current marketing effort is as effective as possible? If you decide to do more, can you find the budget, form a volunteer task force, free up a staff person, or go after *pro bono* (no charge) help? And suppose you do have some real limitations. Can you override them with sheer enthusiasm and commitment?

Here you decide how much your organization can really put into marketing.

4. What are your realistic, attainable action goals? By when?

Having answered the first three questions, weigh the ideal results you would like to achieve against the realities of the marketplace and your internal capabilities. Then decide on your goals and the time frame in which you believe you can achieve them.

*To set your action goals, complete **Section A** of **Worksheet 1**, pages 109–111.*

It may be clear what results you want, but not so clear what you will do to achieve them. The third and fourth marketing steps, **The Marketing Audit** and **The Marketing Plan,** will help you clarify how your goals can be met.

Setting image goals

It is likely you will set an image goal for your marketing effort if you meet at least one of these conditions:

▲ You are a brand-new nonprofit.
▲ Your organization is changing, growing, or adding new programs or services.
▲ Your image is outdated.
▲ You believe people don't understand how you can meet their needs.
▲ You want to maximize your opportunities by being better known in the community.
▲ You want to reinforce your reputation as it stands right now.
▲ You want to differentiate yourself from others.

Unless you are a new group just starting out (in which case you surely have image goals), you already have some kind of reputation. It may be clear or cloudy, accurate or inaccurate, positive or negative. Image goals come into play when you want to increase your visibility or change how you are perceived.

Right now, it may be clear you need a new image. However, you may not be able to describe exactly what that image should be. The next section in this book, **Position Your Organization,** will help you clarify the unique role you want your organization to play and how you want to be seen.

Progress on image goals can be difficult to measure. To evaluate success, watch overall response to your marketing plan; listen for comments and reactions from program participants, board members, funders, and staff; and conduct interviews with key individuals in the community.

Set your sights high

Let's return once again to PWI and look at how it decided to change its image:

Over the years, employers have accepted PWI as a reliable source of qualified people for entry-level positions. It is clear by the types of job postings sent in, however, that employers do *not* view PWI as a source of candidates for positions closer to the top of the organizational chart. This is a growing problem for PWI because its participant population is changing. More and more people come to the agency who are overqualified for entry-level work. PWI's capacity has grown—it can meet a broader range of employers' needs—but its image lags behind. Staff and members of the Advisory Board agree it is necessary to change how the agency is seen.

The image goal: *To be seen as a premier source of qualified applicants for both entry- and management-level jobs.*

---

*To set your image goal, complete **Section B** of **Worksheet 1,** page 112.*

▲▲

SAMPLE

WORKSHEET 1   SET MARKETING GOALS

SECTION A — Action Goals

Complete this worksheet as an individual exercise or include staff and board members. Some people benefit from structured idea-generating techniques such as brainstorming, visualization, and timed writing or drawing to help them set goals. These techniques are described in **Appendix A.**

Instructions
The four steps to setting action goals will help you organize information that should be readily at hand. You may have one or more action goals. Complete the four steps for each of your goals.

1. What are the absolute best results you could hope for? By when?

If you could wave a magic wand, what would appear? (Don't worry if it seems a bit far-fetched. The next steps are designed to bring you down to earth.) If your situation warrants it, try coming up with your ideal for a six-month to three-year period.

Goal: By When:

1. Continue placing 250 people with disabilities   Annually.
   in jobs each year.

Goal: By When:

2. Increase job postings for upper-level positions   1 year.
   from current Employment Committee members from
   an average of 2 per month to 20 per month.

Goal: By When:

3. Add 25 new employers to the Employment Committee   1 year.
   within one year.

2. What outside factors might help or hinder your ability to achieve this ideal?

Goal 1: Continue placing 250 people with disabilities in jobs each year.

Outside factors working **FOR** you: Outside factors working **AGAINST** you:

1. Unemployment remains low in the   1. Seeing "harder to place" candidates
   area, producing high demand for   with more severe disabilities
   qualified candidates.   and/or higher qualifications.

2. Acceptance of people with   2. Middle management is one area where
   disabilities continues to increase.   job market is tightest.

3.   3.

Continued

SAMPLE

SECTION A — Action Goals (continued)

Goal 2: Increase job postings for upper-level positions from current Employment Committee members from an average of 2 per month to 20 per month.

Outside factors working **FOR** you:

1. Regularly get job posting from 150+ employers.

2. Increasing demand nationally for higher-skilled workers.

3. Possible passage of new Americans with Disabilities Act would focus attention on affirmative action for people with disabilities.

Outside factors working **AGAINST** you:

1. Many employers unaware that people with disabilities can perform in upper-level jobs.

2. Hard to change way we are currently seen by employers.

3.

Goal 3: Add 25 new employers to the Employment Committee within one year.

Outside factors working **FOR** you:

1. Hundreds of employers out there we don't currently work with.

2. Advisory Committee members willing to provide contacts.

3. Potentially, Americans with Disabilities Act.

Outside factors working **AGAINST** you:

1. Takes a lot of time to establish relationship with employer.

2. Employers with no track record hiring people with disabilities usually have lots of misconceptions.

3. Some employers already work with other PWIs and related job placement programs.

Continued

24

SAMPLE

SECTION A — Action Goals (continued)

3. How will realities of budget, staff/volunteer time, and other capabilities affect your effort to achieve these results?

What can you handle? How much in the way of time and resources can you really commit to your marketing effort? Note your answers below:

-- Processing more and/or different types of job postings is no problem with current staff and computer systems.

-- Calling on new employers could stress staff.

-- Need to make time to review how we approach employers -- different personnel processes with upper-level positions?

-- One time federal hold over funding is currently available to apply to promotion campaign.

4. What are your realistic, attainable action goals? By when?

Weigh the ideal results you would like to achieve against the realities of the marketplace and your internal capabilities. Then decide on your goals and the time frame in which you believe you can achieve them.

Goal: By When:

1. Continue placing 250 people with disabilities   Annually.
   in jobs each year.

Goal: By When:

2. Increase job postings for upper-level positions   1 year.
   from current Employment Committee members from
   an average of 2 per month to 10 per month.

Goal: By When:

3. Add 20 new employers to the Employment Committee   1 year.
   within one year.

SAMPLE

SECTION B — Image Goals

1. How are you currently seen by the people or groups most important to you?	2. Are you satisfied with this image?	3. How would you like it to change?
A. People you serve:	A.	A.
1. Rehab counselors and people with disabilities view us as an effective job placement resource.	1. Yes, but we're concerned about meeting the needs of a growing number of candidates with advanced degrees and management-level skills.	1. We want to maintain this image and meet emerging needs.
2. Employers, at least those who know us, view us as a good source of entry-level employees.	2. Yes, but we want them to know we can do more.	2. Get employers to see us as a source of management level employees as well as entry level.
B. Others in the community:	B.	B.
Funders see us as an effective provider of an important service.	Yes.	Fine as it is.

*If you aren't sure what your new image should be, the next section in the workbook, **Position Your Organization**, will help you clarify this issue.*

4. How do you want your image to change and with whom? Write your image goal here:

To be seen by employers as a premier source of qualified applicants for both entry- and management-level jobs.

If you are unclear about what your image should be—how you want to be seen by others—then completing Step 2 is important to your marketing effort. Positioning means finding and establishing your niche or unique role in the community. You define *who you are* and *how you want to be seen.*

This chapter walks you through a six-step finding-your-niche process that helps you complete the phrase *"We're the people who_____."* Ideas and suggestions are provided to help you firmly establish your niche.

Step

Position Your Organization

You are in the right place in this book if:

☐ You believe your organization needs to change or clarify its role or image in the community.

☐ You are considering a major shift in emphasis, population being served, methods, or style in your organization or programs.

☐ You want to build understanding of your unique role inside the organization—among staff, board, and volunteers.

Position your organization

Positioning is finding and establishing your niche

Your niche is the distinctive role you play in the community. It is based on your unique ability to make an impact. You position your organization—and build a clear public image—through initial impressions, consistent messages, and delivering high quality programs and services over time.

Here are examples of three nonprofits that have positioned themselves well on a national scale:

▲ **The United Negro College Fund**—Dedicated to opening doors to advanced education for young African-Americans; *"A mind is a terrible thing to waste"*.
▲ **Planned Parenthood**—Front-line advocates and health care providers for reproductive choice.
▲ **Mothers Against Drunk Driving (MADD)**—Crusaders for stronger action against the crime of drunk driving and the leading victim-assistance organization in the nation.

When you have successfully positioned your organization, people recognize who you are and what you do. It makes sense to them. As you build recognition over time you will naturally expand your realm of associations. As a result, the exchanges you seek—and unexpected opportunities—are more likely to come your way. Effective positioning is like arriving at higher ground. It opens whole new vistas for the future.

Positioning Worksheet

There is one worksheet for positioning, **Worksheet 2**. It will guide you through the process of defining your niche. A completed sample copy can be found on page 37 (blank copy on page 113).

A.   Check in with your mission

The positioning statement you develop should be a direct expression of your mission or purpose. A usable mission statement accurately defines what good your organization intends to do and with whom.

If your mission is clear, easily understood, and provides the right sense of direction for the future, you can go on with positioning. If the mission is at all murky or there is disagreement in your group about what it should be, it is important to resolve these issues. You may simply need a rewrite to bring things up to date. Or, it might be necessary to answer some "big questions" about your direction.

When you have successfully positioned your organization, people recognize who you are and what you do. It makes sense to them.

Here is what happened when one organization examined its mission:

Beacon House was founded at the turn of the century. The original mission statement reads, "The purpose of Beacon House is to extend the hand of God's charity to wayward girls and bring infant children into marriages otherwise deprived of this blessing." It provides room, board, and medical care to unwed mothers and places their babies with adoptive families. Over the years, Beacon House stops being a "home for wayward girls" and becomes solely an adoption agency. It continues to offer some counseling for those giving babies up for adoption. By 1970 the mission reads, "To provide adoption services matching waiting children with loving families."

The initial planning meeting for an 80th anniversary celebration touches off a controversy about how to use the event to position the agency. Looking back over its history, some board members and staff are surprised at the original dual focus on mothers and children. They question the organization's current mission, especially in light of increasing numbers of single women choos-ing to keep and raise their babies. The issue escalates into a full-blown examination of the organization's future.

As a result, the group decides to reaffirm their original commitment in a vastly changed contemporary setting. They speed up plans to add new services and take advantage of the anniversary to, in part, change the organization's image. The new mission, as it enters its 80th year, reads, "To support the choices and abilities of single mothers and adoptive parents to provide loving families for children."

In the case of Beacon House, something as "innocent" as an anniversary celebration raised surprisingly provocative questions. In the process of answering them, the organization strengthened its overall foundation, envisioned a broader niche for the future, and provided the direction necessary for its marketing efforts to be as productive as possible.

*Now go to **Section A** of **Worksheet 2,** page 113, to check in with your mission.*

B. Look at needs and how you might address them

Meeting specific needs—both present and future—is the crux of your role in the community and the driving force behind positioning. Because circumstances and conditions aren't static, your organization's role will undergo changes over time.

As you look closely at ongoing and emerging community needs, ideas about how to respond follow naturally. You may decide to strengthen your existing role by adding, dropping, or modifying programs. You might also consider services with entirely new participant groups.

Here is an example of an organization that saw a need and decided to address it:

A rape crisis center in a Midwestern community provides intensive, long-term emotional and medical support to crime victims. The mission is "To empower victims of sexual assault to recover from their trauma and regain their sense of personal security."

After two years of operation, the Center institutes client satisfaction surveys. Emotional and medical services are rated highly, but staff members note a trend in the responses that lead them to identify a "missing link." Women report a lack of technical support for their experiences with the legal system—which range from satisfactory to disastrous. Staff members discuss the issue and conclude that empowerment through legal action is a critical part of the recovery process missing from their program. They decide it would be right to include legal support among the services at the Center.

You needn't address every need you can identify

Many marketing experts counsel organizations against spreading their energies too thin. Conventional wisdom says you will make the greatest impact if you are highly focused and concentrate your energies on being the absolute best at what you do. In other words, aim deep like a laser, not wide like a floodlight.

This doesn't mean you should dismiss growth opportunities or refrain from expanding your services. It does mean you should exercise caution before moving to enlarge your niche.

Here is an example of a nonprofit that saw a need within its mission, but chose not to respond:

A sheltered workshop has operated for 15 years and provides services to adults with severe physical disabilities or mental retardation. The group receives particular attention for their innovative "work crew" program, which brings participants into the community for supported work in nonsheltered sites.

An area hospital noted for its inpatient rehabilitation programs approaches the workshop to cooperate in a vocational program for people with brain injuries. The workshop wrestles with the positioning issue. Should it expand its role to serve a new participant group?

There is heated debate. On the one hand, nobody questions the need for such services and all believe the workshop would be effective putting such a program in place. On the other hand, board members and some staff have been pressing for the workshop to take a stronger advocacy role in housing and other issues affecting their current participants. They believe the new venture would sap energy from these efforts.

A close vote by the board goes against getting involved in the new venture. At the same meeting, the board endorses increased advocacy for the populations already being served.

This could have gone either way. The group was very tempted to expand, but decided that, at least for the time being, the greater contribution would come from intensely focusing their efforts on behalf of their present clientele. They may have been entirely successful in the new endeavor, but chose instead to strengthen their existing niche.

*At this point, turn to **Section B** of **Worksheet 2** (blank copy on page 113) to record the community needs you will address and ideas for how your programs and services might respond.*

C. Survey the competition to see how you fit in

Few nonprofits find themselves facing off in a classic macho showdown. Nonetheless, it is essential to consider whether there is room in town for the unique role you want to play. Are your ideas original? Or are you heading for a niche that is already filled? Should you forge ahead alone? Or might a partnership be more appropriate?

To answer these questions you will need to identify potential competitors and partners to see if what you have in mind is truly a necessary and unique contribution in the community. Your information might come from a variety of sources, but it's important to be discreet. Because your ideas are still in the formative stage, you want to avoid raising expectations or drawing premature attention to your plans.

At this point, you confirm the need for the role you want to play and decide whether you would be most effective teaming up or going it alone. Once you know where you stand, you're ready to draft your preliminary positioning statement.

Turn to **Section C** *of* **Worksheet 2**, *page 114, to assess where you stand with the competition.*

D. Draft your positioning statement

People often ask what the difference is between mission and positioning statements. Your mission should define the specific outcomes your organization is after—what good you intend to do and with whom. It is a statement of *accountability*.

Your positioning statement pinpoints the unique role you want to play in the community. It cites the specific niche you fill and, in very few words, describes how you fill it. It is a statement of *character* and *reputation*.

This step crystallizes your thoughts so far. A strong positioning statement:

▲ Is short and to the point.
▲ Uses everyday language, avoiding technical, insider terms of your field.
▲ Conveys something of the character of your organization.
▲ Has a sense of action.

Let's look again at the three well-positioned organizations from the beginning of this chapter.

▲ **The United Negro College Fund**—Dedicated to opening doors to advanced education for young African-Americans; *"A mind is a terrible thing to waste"*.
▲ **Planned Parenthood**—Front-line advocates and health care providers for reproductive choice.
▲ **Mothers Against Drunk Driving (MADD)**—Crusaders for stronger action against the crime of drunk driving and the leading victim-assistance organization in the nation.

Note how each statement meets the four criteria for effective statements. They are short and to the point, use everyday language, convey character, and imply action.

Here are three tips to help you draft your positioning statement:

1. **Summarize the conclusions you have drawn so far in the positioning process.**
   You now have the basis for your positioning statement. It's helpful to review your findings before you move on.

2. **Generate lots of possibilities.**
   There are many structured methods for developing material for your positioning statement, including *brainstorming, visualization,* and *timed writing* or *drawing.* (See **Appendix A** for more on these idea-generating techniques.) Or, of course, you can simply sit down and have at it.

3. **Beware of writing in a group.**
   Consider assigning the actual writing of the statement to one person or a team of two. Writing as a group, no matter how bright and creative the members, often gives rise to "the lowest common denominator syndrome." The better role for a larger group is generating raw material, reviewing drafts, making limited suggestions, and approving the final wording.

*Now, turn to **Section D** of **Worksheet 2,** pages 115–116, and work through your draft positioning statement.*

E. Test your positioning statement for support

After drafting your statement, you know what *you* believe your niche should be. Most new ideas require some kind of support—financial, moral, political, or all three. Now it is time to confirm the viability of what you want to do with other critical parties.

To test for support, you will prepare a short presentation of your positioning statement and the rationale behind it, identify the three people or groups whose support is most crucial to your future success, and make an appointment to talk with them.

A list of three people or groups is a *minimum.* Go to as many potential sources of support as you feel appropriate. Potential groups for testing include:

▲ Key staff and board members
▲ Funding sources and policymakers
▲ Program participants, opinion leaders, or others who might have a stake in what you do

This is also a good time to seek "sage advice." If you know people whose opinion you respect simply because they are wise or a longtime observer of the scene, ask for their reaction, too.

Here is an example of what one group learned through a visit with a key source of support:

The board of a Neighborhood Development Association meets in anger over the continued operation of a porno shop and movie theater in their area. They have been seen as a quiet group, more noted for rehabbing houses than getting involved in hot issues, but some board members are arguing for change. They work through the steps of positioning and find their "quality of neighborhood life" mission still fits and that there is a clear need that no other organized group is addressing. With a strong sense of momentum, they describe their expanded role as "an activist force ready to confront the obstacles to ridding the area of pornography."

Board leaders arrange a visit with the neighborhood's representative on the City Council. Although the Council Member is sympathetic to the group's goals,

she advises them to "tone down the rhetoric a bit." She says the Council as a whole supports antipornography efforts and that there has recently been discussion of how to better engage residents to work *with* them in developing plans. She offers to set up a meeting with law enforcement officials and suggests the group might enjoy greater support if they position themselves as interested in planning cooperatively, rather than ready for a fight.

By testing their positioning statement, the neighborhood group learned in advance how they might modify their approach to increase support from at least one key quarter. There was some skepticism as to whether they were just being "pacified," but the group decided to try cooperating as an interim tactic before taking a more militant approach.

By testing your statement—and the logic behind it—you are already moving from finding your niche to establishing it. It is important to realize that once you ask for others' opinions, you are beginning to create recognition for the role you want to play.

Now go to Section E of Worksheet 2, page 116, for the specific steps to test your positioning statement.

F. Refine and clarify your niche

To refine and clarify your niche, revise your positioning statement, taking into account the useful feedback you have received. Some reactions may be provocative, challenging you to rethink your approach, more carefully examine risks, or raise your sights even higher. It's rare, if you feel strongly committed to what you have developed, that you will receive no support whatsoever. However, there are ideas that come ahead of their time and evoke outright opposition. It could be you've thought up a real dud, but remember that what is now the League of Women Voters got its start as a radical fringe.

Again, it can be helpful to talk through ideas and possible changes in a group, but return the statement to your writer for final revisions.

Write your revised statement in Section F of Worksheet 2, page 116.

Tips for establishing your niche

1. **Make sure your entire staff, board, and volunteers are aware of your positioning statement and understand what it means for the organization.**
   It's a good idea to reinforce this in a number of ways, such as informal conversations, meetings, memos, and in-house newsletters. Be sure to invite comments from anyone who hasn't been involved to date in the positioning process. Remember, your positioning statement not only provides the basis for the image you project in the community, but serves as an internal tool to help you keep your focus and identity clear.

2. **Continue to "test" your positioning statement with a broader circle of people in the community.**
   There is no more powerful way to build awareness, involvement, and support than by face-to-face meetings.

3. **Make a consistent, public statement.**
   Develop a "boiler paragraph" for your organization and use it in your external publications and promotional materials. A boiler is a description of your organization that is a composite of your mission and positioning statements. It should also include one or two other key points that help build the image you want. Here is a sample boiler:

   > *The Greater Regional Association of Nonprofit Theorists (GRANT) is at the crossroads of philanthropy in the State of Texas, maintaining the most comprehensive and up-to-date database on philanthropic trends. GRANT's research, conferences, and publications help corporate, community and family foundations make the most informed giving decisions possible. Established in 1955 and awarded a Presidential Medal for Community Service in 1987, GRANT is the oldest and largest organization of its kind in the United States.*

   Establishing a niche takes time. To be successful you must reinforce over and over again how you wish to be perceived.

4. **Maintain a presence.**
   Be sure people in your organization join—and are active in—professional networks, clubs, and trade associations in your field. Being a leader among peers increases your visibility and brings recognition and opportunity with it.

5. **Become known by the media.**
   You are an authority in your field. Find out who in the media covers your issues, introduce yourself, and make it clear you are available as an authoritative source.

6. **Take a stand.**
   When issues arise that affect you or those you serve, consider getting right out front with your values and your voice. Number one, it's often the right thing to do. Number two, you'll definitely be noticed.

The single most critical factor in establishing your niche is consistent delivery of top-notch services and programs. There never has been and never will be a substitute for quality.

7. Join leadership networks.

No matter what your specific mission or focus, it is beneficial to your organization to be well known and recognized by community leadership. There are more than 600 organized Community Leadership Organizations in the United States. Many are affiliated with Chambers of Commerce, United Ways or foundations, and some are independent. If you've got one in your town, join up. If not, consider starting one.

8. Form an advisory council(s).

Aside from the extremely beneficial input and guidance you may receive, inviting experts, consumers, and other key people to work with you goes a long way toward establishing a higher profile.

9. Deliver.

The single most critical factor in establishing your niche is consistent delivery of top-notch services and programs. There never has been and never will be a substitute for quality.

There will never be a substitute for quality

SAMPLE

WORSHEET 2   POSITION YOUR ORGANIZATION

SECTION A — Check in with your mission

1. Write your current mission statement here:

Increase employment opportunities for people with disabilities.

    a. Is the mission clear?

       Yes.

    b. Does it still provide the right sense of direction for the future?

       Yes.

2. What changes, if any, should be considered in your mission?

None.

SECTION B — Look at needs and how you will address them

For information to complete this section, turn first to your clients and staff. They're the best sources you have. However, sometimes staff and clients are too close to issues and current programs to see what changes in focus could produce even greater impact. Add some outside perspective, too.

1. List the most critical ongoing or emerging community needs you will address.

Due to greatly improved access to education and adaptive technology, increasing numbers of people with disabilities are qualified to pursue careers formerly closed to them. There will be an ongoing need for employment services to this population. At the same time, business and industry face predicted labor shortages at all but the uppermost levels.

2. Outline ideas for how you might respond.

Increase employer awareness of the capabilities of people with disabilities. More aggressively pursue job placement for candidates with upper-level skills.

Continued

SAMPLE

SECTION C — Survey the competition to see how you fit in

1. Who are your competitors ?

Other PWIs and job placement programs.

For-profit employment services.

2. What are you competing for?

We compete to some extent with other PWIs and placement programs for participants and occasionally for placements.

We compete head-to-head with for-profit firms, but they seldom represent people with disabilities.

3. How do your outstanding strengths compare with theirs?

With 13 years' experience, we have a solid reputation and extensive employer contacts. We are certainly as effective as anyone in the business at placement, but we haven't been quite as strong in public relations. Basically, there are a lot of good agencies, but the demand from both candidates and employers is so strong that we seldom step on each others' toes.

4. List potential partners and how you might team up with each.

Employers -- we already work as "partners" in the placement process with many employers. We will continue to do so and want to expand this network.

Other PWIs and placement groups -- although we have collaborated on some past efforts, at this time it seems best to concentrate on refocusing our own image and role.

Continued

SAMPLE

WORKSHEET 2—POSITION YOUR ORGANIZATION

There are four general ways competition affects decisions on positioning. After surveying the competition, how do things look for you? Check all those that apply:

☐ There are needs to be met and we're exactly the people to do the job.

☐ It will be best to meet needs through a collaborative venture.

☑ Needs we identified are being met to some degree, but our contribution is necessary and unique, so we'll compete. (No one has specifically sought a niche as a PWI placing people in upper-level jobs.)

☐ The needs we identified are being met very well by others; we should back off.

SECTION D — Draft your positioning statement

Your positioning statement should make it easy for people to quickly grasp who you are and what unique role you want to play.

1. **To develop material for your statement, first complete the following phrases in as many ways as you can think of. (Instructions for three structured ways to generate ideas is provided in Appendix A.)**

    a. We're the people who...
    - place people with disabilities in jobs
    - meet employers' needs
    - do it right
    - always follow through
    - dispel myths
    - can match the right person to the right job
    - advocate for people with disabilities
    - open doors for people at upper levels with disabilities

    b. No one but no one can _____ as well as we do.
    - provide professional employment services
    - provide great service
    - do follow-up services
    - introduce employers to qualified candidates who can do the job
    - help generate more opportunity for people with disabilities

    c. We want to be seen as...
    - effective
    - responsive
    - the best at what we do
    - in synch with the times
    - professional/reliable
    - aware of employers' needs
    - a partner in employment success
    - a "first resort" resource

2. **Now go back and circle the phrases that most strongly convey who you are and what unique role you want to play.**

Continued

39

SAMPLE

3. Based on the circled phrases in Section D, and applying the four criteria for positioning statements *(short and to the point, uses everyday language, conveys character, and has a sense of action)*, **write your draft statement here:**

```
PWI: We represent highly qualified people with disabilities who can do the
job at upper levels of business and industry.
```

SECTION E — Test your positioning statement for support

1. List at least three key potential sources of support with whom you will test your positioning statement.

```
Advisory Committee chair

Agency president (formerly directed PWI program)

Area personnel association liaison
```

2. Make appointments with these people or groups and, in each case, gain answers to these four questions:

a. Based on your knowledge of our organization and this community, do you agree this is how we should be positioned?

```
All said yes. Personnel association president invited PWI to make
presentation at next monthly lunch meeting.
```

b. Why or why not?

```
Everyone confirmed the need for us to do more in this area.
```

c. How might we modify our ideas to improve them?

```
Emphasize all levels. Don't lose entry-level niche with new focus.
```

d. Are there other people or groups you would recommend we talk with?

```
Ask for input on "how to get the word out" from full Advisory Committee
and representatives of current Employment Committee.
```

SECTION F — Refine and clarify your positioning statement

Write your revised positioning statement here:

```
PWI: We represent highly qualified people with disabilities who can do the job
at every level of business and industry.
```

In Step 3, you take stock of your current marketing efforts and decide what you might change, add, or improve in order to achieve your goals.

An audit gives you a framework for understanding your marketing challenge. The process points up:

▲ Positive elements you already have in place.
▲ Additional information you need.
▲ Adjustments you should make.
▲ Features to promote.

We recommend you read the entire chapter before beginning the audit.

Step

Conduct a Marketing Audit

You are in the right place in this book if:

☐ You have a marketing goal and want to know how to achieve it.

☐ You have a marketing problem, but can't put your finger on what's wrong.

☐ You are considering a promotion campaign (small-scale or large) and want to be sure it is focused and on target.

Conduct a marketing audit

Marketing goals provide the focus for an audit

If you have *image goals,* the audit will help you see what key groups of people you need to reach and how your marketing effort should be organized to reinforce the image you want.

If you have *action goals,* the audit will help you decide if you have the right product for the right people and how to line up the other elements to produce results.

Conducting an audit

The audit helps you begin aligning the *Six Ps of Marketing—product, publics, price, place, production,* and *promotion.* Having the *Ps* lined up means they relate correctly to each other. It looks like this:

Product	You have a high-quality program, service, or product that meets people's needs.
Publics	You know with whom you're going to exchange the product and its benefits to them.
Price	The price is right—not too high, not too low.
Place	The product is accessible.
Production	You can effectively meet demand.
Promotion	You use strong techniques that motivate people to respond.

Lining up the Ps

The actual amount of time spent on audits varies. Some people use the audit questions to help them quickly zero in on marketing "hot spots." Others prefer to conduct an in-depth assessment involving many people over a considerable length of time. The first audit you do usually requires the most effort; you are learning the process and naturally consider every audit question in depth. Once you are a veteran, your insights will come faster.

If you are looking at a number of individual programs or divisions, it is best to audit each individually. At the very end of this chapter, suggestions are given for putting together an audit summary or report. There, you can point out themes and overarching issues that emerge through the individual audits.

Marketing Audit Worksheets

There are two worksheets for the marketing audit. **Worksheet 3,** blank copy on page 117, contains all the questions for the marketing audit and a series of six *Audit Checkpoints* corresponding to each of the *Six Ps.* At the Checkpoints you stop, determine if each *P* is in line, and check *one or more* of the following:

✔ *Checkpoint*

☐OK ☐Need information ☐Adjustment necessary ☐Feature to promote

---

☐ **OK**

This area is in good shape. There may be features to promote, but there is no need for further information or adjustments.

☐ **Need information**

You can't fully answer the audit questions, or you need other critical information to make sound marketing decisions.

☐ **Adjustment necessary**

There are steps you should take to correct problems or strengthen your marketing effort.

☐ **Feature to promote**

This area offers a particularly attractive feature that you may wish to point up in your promotion efforts.

If you check *need information, adjustment necessary, or feature to promote,* you will then turn to **Worksheet 4,** page 121, to record specific questions, ideas, and concerns that will need to be addressed in your marketing plan. Completed sample copies of both worksheets begin on page 54.

The Checkpoints are a flexible tool. People who are more experienced with marketing may decide to bypass some audit questions and use the Checkpoints alone to test their thinking, confirm how the *Ps* are lining up, and decide what action to take.

THE MARKETING AUDIT

Product

Whether you sell it or give it away, whether it's as visible as neighborhood renewal or its province is the human heart, what your organization offers is a *product*.

Product

What is the product?

Your product is the *something of value* to be exchanged for something you need. To market your product, you have to be able to define it so the people you serve can clearly understand what it is and how it meets their needs. If people don't understand the product, find it difficult to use, or just plain don't like it, some adjustments will be needed as part of your marketing plan.

Here is a definition of a product offered to women on Aid to Families with Dependent Children (AFDC) by a technical school in cooperation with a social service agency:

The product is training in computer programming skills leading to jobs that start at $20,000 per year. Major features include nine months of classroom training, a three-month business internship, and assistance with job placement. Area corporations that employ large numbers of computer programmers are intensively involved with the program.

Is your product in line? Is it of high quality and does it meet a specific need?

In order to make the exchanges you want, the product must meet a specific need of your "customers." And in order to be successful over time, those customers must be satisfied with what they get. To answer this audit question, consider the following:

▲ Are you meeting the needs and expectations of the people for whom the product is intended?
▲ Is there anything about the product or service that makes it difficult to understand or use?
▲ Do your customers give you high marks?

Problems in any of these areas get in the way of satisfying existing customers—and attracting new ones.

If you do find a problem with your product, it is crucial to marketing success that you make the adjustments necessary to solve it.

The computer training program described on the previous page conducted an audit to discover why it was having such difficulty filling its training classes.

After three years of excruciating and exhaustive promotion efforts to fill minimum class goals of only 12 students (out of which all graduates get jobs), the group wants to sort out what is making it so hard to achieve their goal. They appoint a review team to conduct a marketing audit. When looking at product questions, the team sees that the product itself is "wrong" for many potential students. Class entry requirements make it impossible for the majority to ever get started. Successful applicants must score extremely high on computer aptitude and math tests. Because the screening is so stiff, only 1 in every 15 women is accepted.

A comment is made that grabs everyone's attention: "It would be nice if our testing process helped screen people 'in' instead of just screening them 'out.'" The team spends time discussing the stringent entry requirements and wonders about a second training track that would be open to women with slightly lower math and computer scores.

The group looks into the question of a second track as part of their marketing plan. They discover excellent career opportunities in Computer Assisted Design, which calls for different aptitudes than programming. It takes nearly a year to put all the pieces in place, but the group successfully adjusts their product. Enrollment triples.

You may initially experience defensiveness when looking at possible adjustments to your organization's product. It's hard to be objective about the need to change when you are close to your product and have worked so hard to develop it. This is natural, but don't let it put you off. The goal is not just to correct problems, but to build on strengths and discover new and better ways to meet the needs of those you serve.

*Turn to **Section A** of **Worksheet 3**, page 117, to complete the Product portion of the Marketing Audit. Write your questions, adjustments needed, and promotion notes on **Worksheet 4**, pages 121–123.*

Publics

Publics

Your product is *what* you want to exchange. Publics covers *with whom*. A *public* is a group or category of people defined by their common interest in your product. They are your "customers" or "buyers." (*Market segments* or *target markets* are other terms commonly used to describe a *public*.) Program participants, funders, referral sources, public officials, and volunteers are often publics for nonprofit groups.

Your publics have the ability to give you what you need.

It is important to be as precise as possible about publics. The success of your marketing effort depends on pursuing exchange relationships with the *right* people, those who have the ability to respond to your promotional message by giving you what you need.

Who are *your* publics?

The problem with publics is coming up with a manageable list. Most organizations interact with a large number of groups, so how do you narrow the list down? Here is the process:

1. First, brainstorm a list of every public of any importance to you. Then, choose your *primary publics* based on these criteria:

   ▲ The groups with the greatest potential to make exchanges that will help you reach your goals.
   ▲ Those with the greatest need for your product.

   You may choose one, two, three, or more primary publics. If you have very broad marketing goals, the number is likely to be higher. A primary public can be the actual people to be served (women on AFDC in the example on the previous page) or important intermediaries such as referral sources (AFDC case-workers who might recommend the program).

   Those on your brainstorm list who are not primary publics are *background publics,* groups that may be the focus of marketing efforts at another time or simply people to keep updated on what your organization is doing.

Are your publics in line? Do you have the "right" publics and know what benefits you provide?

2. Once you identify your primary publics, it is important to know what each values most about your product. People are motivated to use a product or service because of what they believe it will do for them.

   Defining your product in terms of its most important benefits from the buyer's point of view is the key to an effective promotional message.

   Each of your primary publics may value different benefits of your product. For example, if the product is a buddy program for offenders reentering the community, you may be marketing to potential buddies, offenders, and funders. These three publics would clearly find different benefits of your product most important. Be careful that you take the perspective of *each* public and find out what is important to *them*.

Often, nonprofit groups have a good idea what their publics value, but want to test their assumptions by asking them directly. Information on what motivates your publics can come from a variety of sources, including:

▲ Your own observations.
▲ Market research: interviews, surveys, focus groups, etc. (See **Appendix B** for suggestions on how to do market research.)
▲ What your publics say about themselves.
▲ Opinions of experts and others intimate with your publics.

Knowledge of what motivates your publics may lead to adjustments in the product to ensure it effectively meets their needs. Knowing your publics' priorities, how they express themselves, and what motivates them will also be essential to developing successful promotion. We will address this point further in the **Promotion Campaign** chapter.

*Turn to **Section B** of **Worksheet 3,** pages 117–118, to complete the Publics portion of the Marketing Audit. Write your questions, adjustments needed, and promotion notes on **Worksheet 4,** pages 121–123.*

Price

Every product has a price. In order to attract buyers—and get the most out of each exchange—the price should be right: not too high and not too low.

Price

To price your product correctly, you first need to identify what you are asking your buyers to "pay." In the general marketplace, all of this is about dollars and cents. While grants, ticket sales, tuition, and fees-for-service are common in the nonprofit world, very often what you ask for *isn't* money, but something else. Price can be different in a range of exchanges. If you want a story in the newspaper, you're asking for column inches. If you want a celebrity "name" to be honorary fund drive chair, you are asking for an endorsement.

There are many nonprofit services with no fees to participants—shelter for victims of domestic abuse, financial planning for seniors, blood pressure screening for everyone—to name a few. When you're marketing free services, the price includes *time* and *trust:* people must feel the product is worth the time it takes to participate and you must be able to earn and keep their trust.

Here is an example of a program that was asking too high a price. Its participants didn't see a "good value."

A well-established agency has provided employment services to low-income adults since the days of CETA. The proven service model is based on an intensive three-day workshop before participants go out on interviews. The services are free.

The agency receives government funding to duplicate its services with unemployed low-income youth who are, for whatever reason, out of school. Reaching the new target group is difficult, but job placement statistics with those who do come into the program are superb—more than 90 percent get jobs. Two years into the program, however, enrollments are still startlingly low.

The agency devotes considerable time to a marketing audit. Product and publics appear to be in line. Then

there is the question of price. Counselors comment that perhaps the approach takes too much time and potential participants are scared away by the three-day format. Intake workers echo that view, stating that many kids who come in expect to get a job "that day."

The staff concludes that youth do view their needs in such immediate terms that a three-day commitment is asking too much. Their marketing plan calls for experimenting with a condensed approach that puts youth out on interviews by the second day of the program. The pilot works and the format is permanently changed.

The program correctly sized up a price problem. Three days was simply more time than the youth market could afford for employment services.

Is your price in line? Not too high, not too low?

While most of the emphasis on getting price lined up rightfully concerns avoiding *overpricing*, *underpricing* can also be mistake. Sometimes charging too little can actually devalue your product in the eyes of others while a higher price may encourage commitment. Many nonprofits have found that putting even a minimal charge on otherwise "free" services gives a sense of investment and improves attendance.

Some products are in such great demand, and are perceived to be so valuable, that high prices can be charged. Theaters and concert halls often sell out their best and most expensive seats first, and there are prestigious volunteer programs that require intensive commitments, promise commensurate rewards, and have people lined up for the privilege.

Here are five points to consider when setting a price, especially when what you are asking for is money:

▲ How much does the product actually cost you to produce?
▲ Do some or all of your prospective customers have the means to pay the full cost or even allow you a profit?
▲ Will your customers perceive enough value to pay what you want to charge?
▲ How much do others charge for similar products?
▲ Should you have a sliding fee scale?

Ultimately, price is in the eye of the beholder. If too high, your customer will balk. If too low, you get less than you deserve.

Price as a feature to promote

The fact that many nonprofit programs are offered at little or no cost is often something attractive to emphasize in promotion. When the word "FREE" appears prominently in promotional materials it can have a powerful effect. One program—geared to teen mothers—offered a two-year intensive self-sufficiency program. Its promotion included a mock check with a flash headline announcing, *"$15,000 in Services Could Be Yours!"*

Response to the promotion was tremendous, and many young women who called said they were impressed to know the real value of what the program was offering.

*Turn to **Section C** of **Worksheet 3,** page 118, to complete the Price portion of the Marketing Audit. Write your questions, adjustments needed, and promotion notes on **Worksheet 4,** pages 121–123.*

Place

Place

There is a scene in the 1967 hit movie "The Graduate" in which a middle-aged man sidles up to the shell-shocked Dustin Hoffman during his graduation party and condenses all his worldly advice into one word, *"plastics."* If all the worldly wisdom about marketing and *place* were to be summed up and confided in someone's ear, the secret whisper would be *"Bookmobile."*

The genius of the bookmobile was in seeing that, for many people, coming to the library was unlikely or impossible and therefore books were just going to have to come to them. These little libraries on wheels, which introduced thousands, perhaps millions, of children and adults to the pleasures of borrowing books, have largely been supplanted by branch libraries, which can now be found even in suburban shopping centers. *Place* was once a barrier to libraries being used, a barrier that has now largely been removed.

Place means the actual physical location or your channels of distribution. If people want what you have to offer, but can't get at it, you have a serious marketing problem. Like price, place can also be a feature to promote.

Is place in line? Are you accessible to your publics?

To answer the question, put yourself in the shoes of your publics. Getting to you should be as convenient and barrier-free as possible. If you are off the busline, on the second floor with no elevator, or in a remote part of town, you may be considered inaccessible by your prospective clientele.

Some place barriers are *emotional* and include:

▲ A location in an "unsafe neighborhood."
▲ A location that is "too public"—your participants need anonymity.
▲ A location that is too "ritzy"—people feel out of their element.

The following example shows how place can present a real marketing problem.

The Jewish Family and Children's Service of a mid-sized community finally realizes its dream. A capital drive raises enough money to enable it to sign a long-term lease and refurbish a central suite of offices. After many years scattered about town, its Big Brother/Big Sister program, refugee resettlement effort, elder services division, volunteer coordinators, and family counseling staff will finally be under one roof.

The new offices open with much hoopla and publicity and the energy within the agency seems to multiply tenfold. But after a few months, a disturbing trend is noted. Although a few initial intake sessions are held,

virtually no new families come into the counseling program. Adding to the staff's dismay, three families abruptly terminate their therapy for no apparent reason.

A staff/board group undertakes a marketing audit and quickly decides that "place" is the issue: other than location, nothing has changed. They decide they need more information and, as a first step in their marketing plan, call the three families who have terminated counseling since the move.

The mini-survey provides the clue to the quandary. The first two people contacted say they found the new offices a problem, but don't say more. The mother in the third family is more blunt. "Do you think I want everyone in town to know we have problems? I felt like I was at someone's wedding reception in your waiting room!"

There was a side effect of the new location that the agency hadn't counted on. With so many people coming and going in the centralized office, counseling clients felt uncomfortably exposed. The agency developed options and ultimately decided to disperse therapists back into private offices in order to solve the problem.

The realities of place sometimes inspire nonprofits to shape their entire approach to service. A good example is AIDS education programs that go directly to the streets to ensure that information gets to intravenous drug users. The AIDS people realize their public isn't about to come to them, so they pick up their services and take them right where they can do the job.

When place is a plus

"Free parking!"

"Shakespeare under the stars!"

"Meals on Wheels!"

"On the National Register of Historic Places!"

There may be something about your location or distribution ability that's a real plus. If you are in a particularly convenient spot, offer a special attraction, or "deliver to your door" you may have a feature to tout in promotional efforts.

*Turn to **Section D** of **Worksheet 3,** page 119, to complete the Place portion of the Marketing Audit. Write your questions, adjustments needed, and promotion notes on **Worksheet 4,** pages 121–123.*

Production

When you are marketing a product, it's crucial that you have the ability to meet demand. If you're late, inefficient, or simply can't come through, chances are you'll lose your customer for good. A study by Technical Assistance Research Programs reveals that 26 of every 27 customers who have a bad experience won't complain, and that 90 percent of them won't come back either. [2]

Production

---

[2]A study by Technical Assistance Research Programs cited by Tom Peters, ***Thriving on Chaos*** (New York: Alfred A. Knopf, Inc., 1987), p. 91.

Is production in line? Can you effectively meet demand?

The ability to meet demand may require adequate staff or volunteers, sufficient physical space, enough inventory in stock, well-maintained vehicles that don't break down, good planning, and a smoothly functioning organization. These are management issues. When looking at production from a marketing standpoint, what needs to be raised are the *"what ifs?"*.

▲ *What if* our promotion succeeds beyond our expectations? Will we be able to serve everyone who calls?
▲ *What if* we get all four grants we've applied for? Will we be able to gear up fast enough to keep our promises?
▲ *What if* every show sells out? Will we be able to extend the run?
▲ *What if* it takes a year to build up demand? Can we afford the lean months?

Getting production lined up means being prepared for *"what ifs?"* both the fat and the thin. It's foolish to expect marketing to work miracles and a shame to be unprepared when it does.

Production as a feature to promote

Many nonprofit services meet emergency needs and pride themselves on being able to rise to nearly any occasion. Walk-in counseling, 24-hour crisis hotlines, and the disaster-ready services of the Red Cross are examples of nonprofits whose ability to meet demand are central to what their publics value and need. As long as such production promises are consistently kept, they can be another strong promotional feature.

*Turn to **Section E** of **Worksheet 3,** page 119, to complete the Production portion of the Marketing Audit. Write your questions, adjustments needed, and promotion notes on **Worksheet 4,** pages 121–123.*

Promotion

Auditing the first five *Ps* is like checking to see if your house is in order. Now it's time to look at promotion: how you invite people in. Promotion covers all the ways you communicate in order to create an image and motivate people to make the exchanges you want. It includes the broad categories of sales, advertising, public relations, and a long list of specific techniques, from brochures to the annual holiday open house to your public service announcements on the radio.

Is promotion in line? Do you use effective techniques that motivate people to respond?

To audit your promotion efforts, make a list of the techniques you have used and assess the effectiveness of each. (An annotated list of promotional techniques can be found in **Appendix C**.) A mistaken notion about promotion is that you continually have to take a fresh new approach. On the contrary, a promotional technique that

Promotion

worked once is very likely to work again. It will be helpful to pull together whatever promotional materials you currently have and critique them. Be careful not to get into debates based on individual taste. The three main points to cover are:

1. Has this promotional tool produced good results?
2. Does it convey the image we want?
3. Does it address the right audience and speak to their particular values and needs?

What do you know you want to add, drop, or improve?

In reviewing promotion, as well as the other *Ps*, you may have developed a number of new ideas worth exploring, decided some current efforts just don't work, and noted successful techniques that require adjustments to your image or message. The specifics of selecting and refining promotional tools comes in the ***Promotion Campaign*** chapter, but for now, it is enough to make a general assessment of your promotional efforts.

*Turn to **Section F** of **Worksheet 3,** page 120, to complete the Promotion portion of the Marketing Audit. Note the techniques you want to add, drop, or improve in **Section C** of **Worksheet 4,** page 123.*

WRAPPING UP THE AUDIT

Worksheets 3 and **4** provide the basic information for your marketing plan. Based on what you have found in the audit, you will go on to gain further information, address problems, and develop a marketing plan designed to achieve your goals.

In addition to the worksheets, some groups find it helpful to write a short report or summary that puts audit findings in a narrative form. A report will be especially useful if you have audited more than one program or division. It brings the audit information together and helps you with an overall perspective. A summary report may include:

▲ A general assessment of your current marketing effort.
▲ Themes and overarching issues.
▲ Priorities for the marketing plan.
▲ Particular points of interest.

A summary can also be useful as a progress report to people who participated in the audit and to others interested in your marketing effort. This could include board members, department heads, the executive director, funders, and friends.

▲▲

SAMPLE

WORKSHEET 3   CONDUCT A MARKETING AUDIT

SECTION A — Product—What you offer

1. What is the product?

Prescreened, qualified job candidates.
Training and education on issues of disability and employment.
Follow-up services to ensure job retention.

2. Is there anything about your product that makes it difficult to understand or use?

People may initially think PWI is asking them to do a "favor" by hiring a person with a disability. It's not always easy to understand that we represent qualified people who can do the job as advertised.

We also have to deal with people's hidden fears about people with disabilities.

✔ *Product Checkpoint*—Is your product in line? Is it of high quality and does it meet a specific need?

    ☑ OK   ☐ Need information   ☐ Adjustment necessary   ☑ Feature to promote

Write your questions, adjustments needed, and promotion notes on Worksheet 4.

SECTION B — Publics—Those with whom you want to make exchanges

1. Make a complete list of your publics for each major product or program.

- current Employment Committee members
- Personnel Association members not on employment committee
- industry-specific employers as recommended by Advisory Committee members
- other employers
- people with disabilities
- rehabilitation counselors
- general public

Continued

SAMPLE

WORKSHEET 3—CONDUCT A MARKETING AUDIT

SECTION B — Publics (continued)

2. Choose your primary publics for each product and note the benefits of the product they value most.

Primary Publics	Benefits
Current Employment Committee members	Expanded service from proven resource
Personnel Association members	Meets needs for qualified employees
Industry-specific employers as recommended by Advisory Committee	Prescreening by PWI saves time

✔ *Publics Checkpoint*—**Are your publics in line? Do you have the "right" publics and know what benefits you provide?**

☑ OK   ☑ Need information   ☑ Adjustment necessary   ☐ Feature to promote

Write your questions, adjustments needed, and promotion notes on Worksheet 4.

SECTION C — Price—How much you charge

1. What are you asking for? Dollars and cents or something else?

There are no fees to employers for PWI services. The price is the time it takes to meet with a PWI representative to learn about the program and to get PWI into the employer's routine for sending out job postings.

2. How much do you charge?

Employers often put in extra time with their first disabled employees to learn more about disability and work place issues.

3. Could your customers—or at least some of them—pay more?

Some employers become enthusiastic about PWI and devote considerable volunteer time to the program.

✔ *Price Checkpoint*—**Is your price in line? Not too high, not too low?**

☑ OK   ☐ Need information   ☐ Adjustment necessary   ☑ Feature to promote

Write your questions, adjustments needed, and promotion notes on Worksheet 4.

Continued

SAMPLE

SECTION D — Place—Where the product is available

1. Do people come to you or do you bring your product to them?

We call on employers at their offices. This is expected standard procedure in the employment services industry.

2. Are there any place "barriers" you should address?

Not really, but we always invite employers to tour our facility. Many do, as it is reassuring to them to see how we do things and to meet some of our candidates.

✔ *Place Checkpoint*—Is place in line? Are you accessible to your publics?

☑ OK   ☐ Need information   ☐ Adjustment necessary   ☐ Feature to promote

Write your questions, adjustments needed, and promotion notes on Worksheet 4.

SECTION E — Production—The ability to meet demand

1. Can you effectively meet demand?

This could be a problem if we get requests for too many upper-level candidates or too many people with specific background and skills that do not match our candidates'.

2. What if demand increases—or falls?

We may have to attempt to recruit even more upper-level candidates, but that would be a great problem to have!

If demand falls overall we could consider staff layoffs, however this hasn't happened in 13 years and there is no indication this is about to happen now.

✔ *Production Checkpoint*—Is production in line? Can you effectively meet demand?

☑ OK   ☐ Need information   ☑ Adjustment necessary (possibly)   ☐ Feature to promote

Write your questions, adjustments needed, and promotion notes on Worksheet 4.

Continued

SAMPLE

SECTION F — Promotion—What you do to motivate people to respond

1. **What promotional techniques have you used? (See Appendix C for annotated list of techniques.) Note the effectiveness of each by placing a check in the appropriate column and add any comments you have.**

Technique	Effective	Not effective	Not sure	Comments
In-person sales	X			Most essential to develop relationships with employers
Telemarketing	X			Continuous follow-up
Newsletter		X		Stopped one year ago -- no one noticed -- no effect on placements
Group presentations	X			Raises awareness of disability issues
Brochure	X			Good general explanation of PWI -- won't do much for current goals
TV PSA	X			Out of use now -- three years ago got 12 new Employment Committee members
Networking	XX			Current Emp. Comm. members often provide "hot leads"
Recognition events	X		X	Employers seem pleased about awards -- get newspaper coverage

✔ *Promotion Checkpoint*—Is promotion in line? Do you use effective techniques that motivate people to respond?

☑ OK   ☐ Need information   ☑ Adjustment necessary

Write your questions, adjustments needed, and promotion notes on Worksheet 4.

SAMPLE

WORKSHEET 4 — INFORMATION & ADJUSTMENTS

SECTION A — Information needed

If you checked *need information* in any of the sections on Worksheet 3, write the specific questions you want answers to below:

1. In what industries and/or large corporations is there greatest demand for middle- and upper-level candidates?

2. How do skills of available job candidates match with business and industry needs?

3. Need lists of companies to contact.

4. Need names of appropriate people to approach in new companies.

5.

6.

7.

8.

9.

10.

Continued

SAMPLE

SECTION B — Adjustments necessary

If you checked *adjustment necessary* in any of the sections on Worksheet 3, note the specific problems needing attention below:

1. Need to revise presentations to include more information and focus on potential of people with disabilities to be upper level employees.

2. Need to work on mailing lists and employer database to ensure we are matching candidates' skills with needs of specific employers.

3. Need to look at membership of Advisory Council to be sure industries with high demand for upper-level candidates are represented.

4.

5.

6.

7.

8.

9.

10.

Continued

SAMPLE

SECTION C — Promotion notes

If you checked *feature to promote* in any of the sections on Worksheet 3 or have other ideas on promotion that come up during the audit, elaborate below:

1. Important to emphasize that people with disabilities are really qualified for all level jobs.

2. PWI meets your needs for qualified employees.

3. No charge to employers.

4. Check out Nebraska campaign we saw at national convention -- borrow materials?

5. Continue in-person sales and tap existing network for leads.

6. Would be good to have coordinated effort to change image -- new PSA, direct mail, billboards, etc.

7. Special brochure for this purpose?

8.

9.

10.

Once you've completed the audit, you know where your current marketing effort is in good shape and what needs to be changed. In the marketing plan you lay out how the *Six Ps* should be aligned in order to achieve your marketing goals.

To develop your marketing plan, you restate your goals, address problems, and conduct research to decide how the *Ps* should line up. Then you develop steps for implementation. More detailed information and guidance on promotion strategy is contained in the next chapter, The Promotion Campaign.

Note: Some situations call for fast action and only a minimum of planning is possible. Even in such cases, before you put a marketing plan together, an abbreviated audit is strongly advised.

You are in the right place in this book if:

☐ You have completed a marketing audit and are ready to put together your overall marketing plan.

Step

Develop a Marketing Plan

Develop a marketing plan

A blueprint

A marketing plan is the blueprint you intend to follow in order to achieve your goals. If you are planning for existing programs, the plan will incorporate the strengths of your current effort with needed changes and improvements. If the plan is for a brand new product, it will pull all the elements together for an effective start on marketing.

At this point, you may keep the goals you set earlier or revise them based on newly gained perspectives. You then specify how the *Six Ps* line up: what product you will market; to whom; how price, place, and production fit in; and an outline of your approach to promotion. Finally, you detail the concrete steps you will take to implement your plan, including responsibilities, deadlines, and budget.

Marketing Plan Worksheet

There is one worksheet for the marketing plan, **Worksheet 5,** page 125. A completed sample copy can be found on page 68.

If you are looking at marketing for a number of programs, divisions, or individual products, it is best to complete the first two sections of **Worksheet 5** for each. At that point, you may wish to combine your plans and develop a master approach to implementation—or you may choose to implement each plan separately.

A marketing plan is the blueprint you intend to follow in order to achieve your goals.

THE MARKETING PLAN

Marketing goals

Your goals provide the focus for the overall marketing effort and therefore belong at the top of any marketing plan. You may have set goals in Step 1 of this book. Refer back to your goals now and respond to this question:

Based on information and perspective gained since these goals were set, are they still right? If not, how should the goals be revised?

*Now, turn to **Section A** of **Worksheet 5,** page 125, and restate the goals for your marketing plan.*

The plan

Before drafting your plan, you may need to answer questions or address problems identified in the audit (**Worksheets 3** and **4**). At this point you have a choice. One option is to go ahead and do some research before starting on the marketing plan. This is recommended if the audit left you with major uncertainties about the needs and values of your publics or the source of any marketing problems. If you believe you already have adequate information, go ahead and start on the plan right now.

Here is an example of a group that took time to get some answers before drafting their marketing plan:

A church-affiliated morning nursery school conducts a marketing audit in an effort to determine why it can't meet its action goals for enrollment in the program. The issue is particularly troubling as many day-care centers in the area have long waiting lists.

It appears there is a product problem—everything else seems to be in line. Before the group can put the "right" product into a marketing plan, they need some answers. Over the next month, volunteers conduct follow-up interviews with the 20 people who inquire about the nursery school but don't enroll. A consistent issue emerges: people like the school, but are looking for a full-day program. The fact that the nursery school op-erates only in the morning makes it out of the question for single mothers and dual-income families—precisely the family profiles that have been growing in the area.

Now that the problem is clear, the group can respond by changing the product to make it more in line with what their "customers" value and need. They also re-search a fair price for a full-day program, calculate increased costs vs. revenue, and make sure their space in the church is available for additional hours.

Before it could draft its plan, the nursery school needed to conduct some basic *market research*.

If you are at a stage where research would provide needed insights, see **Appendix B** for more information on types of market research and how to proceed.

Draft your plan

By now you have learned a great deal about how the *Six Ps* should line up in an effective marketing plan. *Now, turn to **Section B** of **Worksheet 5**, pages 125–126, and fill in the elements of your marketing plan.*

Many groups find it beneficial to gain feedback on their draft marketing plan. If you believe it will be helpful, ask other staff, your executive director, board members, a marketing professional, or others to look over the plan and identify any problems or suggest ideas to improve it.

Here is the marketing plan for the church nursery school:

Goal: Increase overall enrollment from 40 to 60 children within 18 months.

1. The product is:

A Monday–Friday nursery school and day-care program, open 7:30 AM–6:00 PM for children two to five years old. Half-day and full-day registration is welcome.

Comments:

Big change!

2. It is being marketed to these primary publics who value particular benefits of the product:

Primary Publics	Benefit	Comments:
Church members.	A safe, loving place for kids that emphasizes religious values.	Church members receive priority in filling available slots.
Families who live in the area surrounding the church (potential users).	A safe, loving place for kids that is convenient.	
Day-care placement and referral services.	A high-quality program they can refer to with confidence.	

3. At this price:

$55.00 per week half time.
$100.00 per week full time.

Comments:

Limited scholarships available to church members.

4. Available at this (these) location(s):

In the church building.

Comments:

Location gives feeling of confidence and security.

5. To effectively meet demand we will:

Increase paid staff and pursue greater volunteer involvement from church membership.

Comments:

New church board president has grandchild in school.

6. The major features to promote are:

High-quality program, low teacher-to-student ratio, reasonable price, religious values are taught, new hours.

Comments:

Growing interest in values education is helpful trend.

Our basic approach to promotion includes:

Continue to promote in church bulletin, encourage word-of-mouth among families currently enrolled, develop and distribute new brochure.

Comments:

Ask parents for other ideas.

Implementation

The marketing plan may paint a picture very different from how things look right now or reflect the need for just a few minor adjustments. Implementing the plan means it is time to take your blueprint and begin construction.

*In **Section C** of **Worksheet 5,** page 127, you decide on implementation steps, assign responsibility, set deadlines, and confirm budgets.*

1. Decide on steps.

In this section, you outline the major tasks that need to be accomplished in order to implement the plan and achieve your marketing goals. It may be helpful to refer again to **Worksheet 4** from the marketing audit. Are there questions and problems that still need to be addressed in order to make your marketing plan a reality? What else needs to be done?

Here are steps the church nursery school needed to take to implement its plan:

1. Get provisional permit and file for permanent change in licensure under state guidelines.
2. Decide date new hours will start.
3. Recruit staff and volunteers to cover extended hours.
4. Set up volunteer training sessions.
5. Develop in-house flyer to announce new hours and survey families currently enrolled to determine how many will register for full day.

6. Write news article for church bulletin and neighborhood paper.
7. Inform day-care placement and referral services.
8. Develop and distribute new brochure.
9. Plan all-school party for first day with new hours.

---

2. Assign responsibility.

Determine who will take responsibility for ensuring that each step in the marketing plan is accomplished. Being responsible for a step may lead to putting together a committee, hiring or finding outside help, or delegating parts of the job to other appropriate volunteers or staff.

3. Set deadlines.

Before you fill in your deadlines, decide what the priorities are. Some steps may be urgent or naturally come first in line. If you are doing marketing planning for a special event or need things in place in time to open a new program or show, then deadlines are already set. Other situations are more flexible.

Many nonprofit professionals juggle marketing with other responsibilities. Be as realistic as possible and make commitments you can keep.

4. Confirm the budget.

Some of the steps in your plan may have associated costs. Make sure those responsible know the parameters of their budgets.

*Now, complete **Section C** of **Worksheet 5,** page 127, **Implementation.***

If your marketing plan calls for significant work on promotion, the following chapter provides a helpful guide to more detailed planning.

Tips for implementing the marketing plan

1. **Have a clear chain of command.**
   Take care to decide who has the responsibility and authority to make decisions. Sometimes a group consensus is necessary. Other times it needlessly holds things up. Define at the outset what will work for you.

2. **Keep people updated and involved.**
   People strongly affected by the plan should already be involved, but make sure *everyone* in the program or organization—as well as other key individuals—are aware of your marketing efforts. This creates additional support for the plan and often leads to unexpected ideas and helpful connections.

3. **Keep communication flowing among all those implementing the plan.**
   If more than one person is implementing the plan, make sure everyone on the team is updated on each others' progress. Changes in scheduling and timing need to be communicated all around.

4. **Be flexible and responsive.**
   Sometimes problems just aren't apparent until implementation is under way. If necessary, stop, regroup, and revise your plan. New ideas and opportunities also can pop up. Be open to expanded horizons!

5. **Evaluate and update regularly.**
   Be sure to regularly evaluate progress toward your goals. If things are working well, stay the course. If your situation changes, take time to update the plan.

If necessary, stop, regroup, and revise your plan

SAMPLE

WORSHEET 5   DEVELOP A MARKETING PLAN

SECTION A — Marketing goals

Write your marketing goals here:

1. Continue placing 250 people with disabilities in jobs each year.

2. Increase job postings for upper-level positions from current Employment Committee members from an average of 2 per month to 10 per month.

3. Add 20 new employers to the Employment Committee within one year.

SECTION B — The plan

1. The product is:

-Prescreened, qualified job candidates.
-Training and education on issues of disability and employment -- emphasis on fact that people with disabilities can perform at all levels.
-Follow-up services.

Comments:

Important to stress that we provide candidates for all level jobs, but we want to make a point about upper level at this time.

2. It will be marketed to these primary publics who value particular benefits of the product:

Primary Publics	Benefit	Comments:
-Current Emp. Comm. members	Qualified employees	
-Personnel Assoc. members	" "	
-New prospects as identified by Advisory Committee	" "	

Continued

SAMPLE

SECTION B — The plan (continued)

3. At this price:

No fees.

Up-front time commitment, particularly with 1st placement.

Comments:

Needs to be presented as a good investment.

4. Available at this (these) location(s):

Appointments and interviews arranged at convenience of employer.

Comments:

We go anywhere.

5. To effectively meet demand we will:

Watch closely how candidates' qualifications match needs of employers.

Comments:

6. The major features to promote are:

PWI can meet your needs for qualified candidates for all level jobs. We follow up and provide all necessary support.

Comments:

We need to be careful here that we don't promise something we can't deliver. We need to be ready to network with rehabilitation system to help ensure that people are trained for high-demand occupations.

Our basic approach to promotion will include:

A staged approach using new materials, some mass media, telemarketing, and our best proven techniques -- networking and in-person sales.

Comments:

Four-color materials from Nebraska are available and will suit our needs nicely. Big cost savings by using their stuff.

Continued

SAMPLE

SECTION C — Implementation

Step	Responsibility	Deadline	Budget
1. Get reaction/input to marketing plan at next Advisory Board meeting.	PWI Director	June 1	
2. Research skills profiles of current group of candidates and make projections for matches with various industries.	Staff	August 1	
3. Research high-demand industries.	Staff	August 1	
4. Develop prospect list with input from Advisory Board.	PWI Director	August 1	
5. Get keylines and negatives from Nebraska to show to Advisory Board and printer.	PWI Director	June 1	UPS charges approximately $50 for both ways
6. Draft more detailed promotion plan with input from Advisory Board.	PWI Director	September 1	

Whether small-scale or large, promotion campaigns include all the ways you communicate in order to create an image and motivate people to respond. In this step, you consider the images, messages, and techniques that make up a promotion campaign.

For some organizations, the basic approach to promotion outlined in the marketing plan is sufficient to move forward. For those putting greater emphasis on promotion, this chapter maps out a detailed process of determining the right image and message, introduces 27 promotion techniques, and provides guidance on choosing the elements for a coordinated promotion campaign.

Step 5

Develop a Promotion Campaign

You are in the right place in this book if:

☐ Your marketing plan calls for changes or additions in promotion.

☐ You want to increase the effectiveness of your current promotion campaign.

Develop a promotion campaign

Inviting people in

Everything in the marketing process is important, but promotion, for many people, is the exciting part. That's natural because promotional activities *themselves* are rewarding. Producing a great new brochure, putting on an event, and making a "sales call" to an important referral source are tangible accomplishments. And when these activities produce the desired results, it's time for celebration!

In developing a promotion campaign you'll need to clarify your organization's image, determine your message, decide what techniques you'll use, and then implement the plan.

Promotion Worksheet

Worksheet 6, page 129, will take you through the four areas of decision-making for promotion. A completed sample copy can be found on page 80.

Promotion conveys an image

Promotional techniques are like ambassadors from your organization. An encounter with them is really an encounter with you. The experts disagree on exact figures, but place the average number of promotional messages we're exposed to daily at somewhere between 560 and 1,800.[3] With such tremendous competition for attention and so little time to make an impact, your promotion has to say something, say it well, and say it fast. It has to create an initial reaction that draws people in, that says, "This is good. This could be for me."

That first impression is created through *image*—the combination of words, pictures, shapes, colors, and sounds that represent your product and your organization.

In today's fast-paced, market-driven world, nonprofits are no different than anyone else in the competition for attention. There is every reason for the nonprofit mission to evoke passionate images that make compelling and lasting impressions.

Defining your image

An effective image says what you'd like it to say, captures your uniqueness, and stands out in a crowd.

To define your image for promotion, write a list of colorful and descriptive words or phrases that best describe how you would like to be seen. If you have developed a positioning statement, it can be helpful to review it at this point.

Promotion techniques are like ambassadors from your organization. An encounter with them is really an encounter with you.

---

[3] ***Star Tribune, Newspaper of the Twin Cities,*** May 19, 1989.

Here is an example of such a list for an alternative school:

- Teachers relate well to kids—great sense of humor
- A necessity in the community
- Cutting edge, risk-takers
- Really *there* for people

- Multicultural
- Quirky
- Passionate about good education
- High quality

Once you have your list, choose which items do the best job of describing the image you would like for your organization or product. Don't worry if the top items don't fit perfectly together or even if there seem to be contradictions. An image can be multifaceted.

*Go to **Section A** of **Worksheet 6**, page 129, to define your image.*

Image doesn't stand alone. It goes with your *message*. At this point, let's go on to consider your message, then we will see how the two work together.

The right message helps produce the response you want

An effective promotional message motivates your audience to take a specific action, and promises a desirable benefit if they do.

The overall message promoting any given product should be consistent. However, since you may be seeking different responses from specific publics, some aspects of your message may change. For example, if your product is counseling for adolescents with behavior disorders, you will speak differently to professional referral sources than to parents.

No matter who you are addressing, your message should be in the everyday language of that audience and contain the essential information they need in order to respond.

You have already laid the groundwork for your message by learning about your publics. There is one more decision to make about message and that is *what specific response you want.* That may seem obvious—you want enrollments, or purchases of season tickets, referrals, the donation, or agreements to volunteer. Those are ultimately the sorts of things nonprofits want, but before you get them, there are a number of preliminary steps.

Your promotional message should specifically ask your audience to take the next step.

For example, a woman on AFDC may have a hard time envisioning herself as a computer programmer steering a corporate vice-president through a planning process—a situation she might actually find herself in after a year long training and placement program. It's too big a leap. However, she *may* easily see herself making a no-obligation phone call to learn more about opportunities for decent-paying jobs.

The appropriate promotional message doesn't just emphasize the long-term benefits of enrollment in the whole program. It sells the *first step* of making a phone call to reserve a place at an informational meeting.

The key to "getting them on the phone" is the *promise of a benefit*. David Ogilvy is the founder of Ogilvy & Mather, one of the three largest advertising agencies in the world. In his 1983 book, **Ogilvy on Advertising,** he writes:

> *Advertising which promises no benefit to the consumer does not sell, yet the majority of campaigns contain no promise whatever. (That is the most important sentence in this book. Read it again.)* Only last year Starch** reported that advertisements with headlines that promise a benefit are read by an average of four times more people than advertisements that don't. [4]*

> ** Ogilvy's emphasis*
> *** "Starch" refers to the Starch Readership Service, an organization that provides factor analyses on adverstising.*

Based on this approach, here is a headline for a flyer aimed at women on AFDC who might be candidates for a computer training program:

Attention Recipients of AFDC —
One Phone Call Could Mean $20,000 a Year!

Contrast the above headline with a more traditional approach:

Attention Recipients of AFDC —
Enroll Now in Our One-Year Computer Training Classes!

The first headline asks for a simple next step and promises the potential of a valuable reward. The second asks for too much too soon and lacks any promise at all.

With either headline, the flyer would go on with more specific information and, if convincing enough, produce calls. Then it is up to the person who answers the call to handle it well, encourage the caller to take the *next* step, and so on.

[4] David Ogilvy, **Ogilvy on Advertising** (New York: Crown Publishers Inc., 1983), p. 160

Answering these five questions will help you craft an effective promotional message:

1. In two or three sentences, describe the average people for whom your message is intended. What are their special circumstances and sensitivities?
2. What specific action do you want people to take as a result of your message?
3. In terms of importance to your target audience, what are the top benefits you offer?
4. What barriers or resistance to your promotional message might you have to meet and overcome?
5. What is your message?

*Turn to **Section B** of **Worksheet 6**, pages 129–130, and record your answers to the above questions.*

You now have the essential image and message to be conveyed through your promotion campaign. This will form the basis for what any promotional techniques should say and, if they are something you can *see* (such as brochures, videos, or refrigerator magnets), how they should look.

The next step is deciding what promotional techniques you will use in your campaign.

It may be 'the information age,' but there is still no substitute for the trust, respect, and cooperation that can be built on a person-to-person basis.

Promotional techniques

Promotional techniques are the actual tools you use to convey your image and message. Your promotion campaign may be modest, employing one or two techniques. Or, you may use a more complex promotion mix with a dozen techniques or more. Regardless of the size of your promotion campaign, always keep in mind the value and importance of personal contact between all those associated with your organization and your many publics. It may be "the information age," but there is still no substitute for the trust, respect, and cooperation that can be built on a person-to-person basis.

Following is a list of promotional techniques used by many nonprofits. You can find an annotated version of this list—with comments on each technique—in **Appendix C.**

Promotional Techniques

Advertising	**Newsletters**
Annual reports	**Posters**
Atmosphere and Attitude	**Public Speaking**
Billboards	**Publishing Articles and Reports**
Brochures	**Radio Public Service Announcements**
Celebrity Endorsements	**Special Events**
Direct Mail	**Specialty Advertising**
Direct Sales	**Talk Shows**
Editorials	**Telemarketing**
Feature Stories	**Television Public Service Announcements**
Letters to the Editor	**Trade Fairs**
Networking	**Videos**
News Conferences	**Word of Mouth**
News Releases	

Following are seven principles to help you choose an effective combination of techniques for your campaign effort.

1. **Gear the tools to the audience.**

   Think about how your audience lives, where they go, what they are most likely to look at, listen to, or read. Then think about the tools that fit into that picture. Three examples:

   a. You might develop the all-time best newspaper ad, but if you want to reach teenagers, you're probably better off with a public service announcement on MTV.

   b. If you want the attention of employers, a brochure for something that looks like "another government program" is probably less effective than something "business like," for example a personally addressed and signed business letter with a snappy preprinted Rolodex card enclosed.

   c. Politicians respond to credible expressions of public opinion. If your audience is the state legislature, editorials in your leading newspapers that showcase your work or back up your point of view can be very persuasive.

2. **Plan how each tool can be used to the maximum effect.**

   In the example above of a newspaper editorial, the effect is wasted if the legislators don't see it. In this case, the nonprofit should make copies (with permission) and be sure to get them where they need to be. It might also enlarge the editorial to poster size and hang it in the lobby, bring it along to conferences, or present it as a gift to others who would value it.

   Here's a critical issue that people often miss: think right up front about how you will *use and distribute* every tool, especially printed pieces like flyers, posters, and brochures. Will you mail them? What mailing list will you use? Will you hire a fleet of high-school kids to tape them up throughout the neighborhood? How else can you get them where they need to go?

Think about how you'll use and distribute every tool

3. **Pick the right mix of techniques—within your budget.**

   In other words, try not to put all your eggs in one basket. You may have your publics targeted with extreme precision, but even within a narrow group people have different learning styles and respond best to different approaches. Think about commercial advertising. When a big campaign is underway, you might have the impression the message is *everywhere*. Nonprofits aren't General Motors or General Mills, but you may be able to back up your brochure with follow-up phone calls, a few well-placed billboards, notices in the newspaper, a personal visit, or a presentation at a conference or public forum.

4. **Repeat your message frequently over an extended period of time.**

   This goes along with picking the right mix of techniques. Beside using a number of tools, reinforce your promotional message as often as you can as long as you can. There is an advertising formula that goes like this: ***Frequency over Time = Reach.*** It means that in order for the average person to really "get" a promotional message it must be repeated over and over again.

5. **If it worked, do it again.**

   During your audit, you listed aspects of promotion that worked for you in the past. Updating your image and message is important in order to stay with the times and accurately reflect your change and growth. But when you have gotten good response from a particular combination of tools, keep using your winning formula. When response begins to decline, then it is time to consider a new approach.

6. **Don't abandon the basics.**

   Some nonprofits have been seduced by glamour or thrown off track by success. They have been smart enough or lucky enough—or both—to get extensive media coverage, a hot pro bono advertising campaign, or have in some other way "struck it rich." It's great to be the talk of the town and it's certainly all for the best, but it can make the routine aspects of your promotion campaign seem tedious and unnecessary. No matter how well things seem to be going, never assume you've got it made. Keep attending to your basic promotion program.

7. **Stay the course.**

   Occasionally a promotion idea will flop. If that happens, try to understand what went wrong, then move on. It is more likely your promotion campaign will produce modest success, falling somewhat short of your goals. Remember that most successful marketing efforts represent a long-term investment. If your goals are realistic, the marketing plan sound, and your promotion well conceived, you should be able to earn the response you want over time. The motto of Ray Kroc, founder and architect of the McDonald's empire was, simply, *"Persistence."*

Given tight nonprofit budgets, you probably can't do everything in the way of promotion you would like to. Make your choices based on what you believe will best help you meet your marketing goals. Be sure to utilize as many free and low-cost techniques as possible.

Decide what techniques to include in your promotion campaign

Some elements of the campaign may already be in place or be fairly easy and inexpensive to undertake. Others ideas may require extensive groundwork, coordination, or fundraising. What nonprofits actually decide to do is often influenced greatly by how much money is available. Be conscious of cost as you choose your promotional tools.

Once you decide on the techniques to be used in your promotion campaign, you may seek outside help from graphic designers, writers, or other communications professionals. If you do, the information from **Worksheet 6** will provide essential direction to get them started. If you are planning to do it yourself, see tips and principles to follow in **Appendix D**.

*Go to **Section C of Worksheet 6,** page 131, choose your promotional techniques and note how they will work together to gain the response you want.*

Implementation

Implementing the campaign includes production of materials and follow-through on using each technique. Responsibility for implementation should be decided and deadlines and budgets set. (See **Step 4,** page 66, for explanations of assigning responsibility and setting deadlines and budget.) Those responsible can then develop individual schedules for meeting deadlines in the plan. Be realistic about how long production really takes and be sure to budget time for things that need to be coordinated—such as engraving plaques for the recognition dinner.

*Now complete **Section D** of **Worksheet 6**, page 132, **Implementation**. See* **Appendix D** for tips on implementing your promotion plan.

▲▲

SAMPLE

WORKSHEET 6 DEVELOP A PROMOTION CAMPAIGN

SECTION A — Image

An effective image says what you'd like it to say, captures your uniqueness, and stands out in a crowd.

1. **Write a list of colorful and descriptive words or phrases that best describe how you would like your organization to be seen:**

   -Businesslike and professional
   -Effective
   -In touch with the times
   -Progressive
   -"Not a charity"
   -Never patronizes people with disabilities
   -Corporate
   -Sense of humor

2. **Circle the above items that do the best job of describing the image you would like for your organization or product.**

SECTION B — Message

An effective message motivates your audience to take a specific action and promises a desirable benefit if they do.

1. **In two or three sentences, describe the average person for whom your message is intended. What are their special circumstances and sensitivities?**

   Human resource professionals in large corporations and managers or owners of smaller businesses. These people are in the business world -- they have bottom line concerns, are often extremely busy, and are regularly approached by employment representatives.

Continued

SAMPLE

WORKSHEET 6—DEVELOP A PROMOTION CAMPAIGN

SECTION B — Message (continued)

2. What barriers or resistance to your promotional message might you have to meet and overcome?

```
-Misperceptions about people with disabilities
-People thinking we are asking them to do us a "favor"
-Fear of the unknown
-Employees initially think we charge for our services
```

3. What specific action do you want people to take as a result of your message?

```
-Agree to schedule time for us to meet with them at their office to learn more
 about PWI and consider joining the Employment Committee
-Call us for more information
-Existing Employment Committee members -- send postings for upper-level jobs
```

4. In order of importance to your target audience, what are the top three benefits and features you offer?

```
1. Qualified candidates
2. Follow-up support
3. Information on disability-related issues
```

5. What is your message?

```
We have people who can do the job you need done
```

Continued

WORKSHEET 6—DEVELOP A PROMOTION CAMPAIGN

SECTION C — Techniques

The principles for an effective combination are: 1) Gear tools to the audience 2) Plan how each can be used to maximum effect 3) Pick the right mix—within budget 4) Frequency over time equals reach 5) If it worked, do it again 6) Don't abandon the basics 7) Stay the course. Make the choices you believe will be most effective, keeping in mind budget constraints and how much effort you can realistically put into development and follow-through.

1. **Check the techniques that you would like to combine in a promotion campaign.**

☐ Advertising
☐ Annual reports
☑ Attitude and Atmosphere
☑ Billboards
☑ Brochures
☐ Celebrity Endorsements
☑ Direct Mail
☑ Direct Sales
☐ Editorials
☐ Feature Stories
☐ Letters to the Editor
☑ Networking
☐ News Conferences
☐ News Releases

☐ Newsletters
☐ Posters
☑ Public Speaking
☐ Publishing Articles and Reports
☐ Radio Public Service Announcements
☐ Special Events
☑ Specialty Advertising
☐ Talk Shows
☑ Telemarketing
☑ Television Public Service Announcements
☐ Trade Fairs
☐ Videos
☑ Word of Mouth

2. **How will these techniques work together to produce the response you want?**

The campaign materials will bear a repeated "take action" message backed up by a single photo image. The telephone campaign will follow the other techniques to reach a specifically targeted group of employers to encourage their participation in the Employment Committee. Individual sales calls will then be made on leads qualified by phone.

A sample of the actual PWI brochure is shown on pages 84–85.

Continued

SAMPLE

WORKSHEET 6—DEVELOP A PROMOTION CAMPAIGN			

SECTION D — Implementation

Step	Responsibility	Deadline	Budget
1. Get estimates on design and production of 5,000 four-color brochures, 5,000 envelopes, 7,500 specialty four-color calling cards, and 15-25 billboards (using Nebraska's four-color separations)	PWI Director	October 1	$6,200
2. Follow up on tip from Nebraska people to get television public service announcement from San Francisco group	PWI Director	October 1	$75 to produce custom trailer with our phone number
3. Firm up, code, and enter mailing lists	Administrative Assistant	January 1	
4. Recruit current Employment Committee members for telemarketing effort	PWI Director/ Advisory Board Chair	January 1	
5. Print materials finished and delivered	PWI Director	January 15	Within budget as above
6. Billboards set to go up February 1	PWI Director	Signed contracts by December 15	
7. PSAs set to run beginning February 1	Administrative Assistant	Delivered to TV stations by Dec. 1	
8. Direct mail brochure and specialty card received by employers	Administrative Assistant	February 10	$300 postage
9. Telemarketing completed	PWI Director	March 15	
10. Sales calls completed	PWI Director/ Staff	June 1	

The following is a black-and-white reproduction of PWI's four-color direct mail brochure. **Front cover:**

Back cover (note use of boiler paragraph and endorsements by listing Advisory Board members):

MULTI RESOURCE CENTERS PROJECT WITH INDUSTRY

MRC/PWI is a partnership of business, industry, and rehabilitation professionals dedicated to improving employment opportunities for people with disabilities. Since 1977, MRC/PWI has worked with over 200 Twin Cities employers and placed nearly 3000 people with disabilities in jobs. Members of the MRC/PWI Employer Advisory Board are:

Terry Bailey
Midwest Federal

Bob Berlute
Multi Resource Centers

Paul Brunelle
Tennant Company

John Burns
Radisson Hotel Corporation

Shelley Chucker
Multi Resource Centers

Carol Dunlap
Electronic Industries Foundation

Jean Fountain
Pillsbury Company

Bill Gjetson
Caterpillar, Incorporated

Joanne Gruen
Deluxe Check Printers

Bruce Hebeisen
MTS Systems Corporation

David King
Electronic Industries Foundation

Ruf North
Rosemount

Joan Orke
Honeywell

Susan Oven
Dayton Hudson

Mary Riley
First Bank System

Steven Ross
AAA

Jim Roth
Multi Resource Centers

Jan Thompson
Division of Rehabilitation Services

Kern Walker
Kurt Manufacturing

MRC/PWI
1900 Chicago Avenue South
Minneapolis, MN 55404

612/871-2402

Inside panels:

You bet he can.

People with disabilities are doing the job at every level of business and industry. Companies who hire them know.

So do we. We're Multi Resource Centers Project with Industry — MRC/PWI for short — and we place qualified people with disabilities in jobs every day.

Our pre-screened candidates have the skills you require. We provide consulting on disability related issues and follow-up is available in any way you need.

If you're looking for people who can do the job, call us today.

MRC/PWI
871-2402

In marketing, like so many things, experience is the best teacher. Regularly evaluate your marketing efforts to learn from experience and keep your efforts on track.

Here are five questions that may help with your evaluation:

1. Did you meet your goals?
2. What worked well?
3. What didn't work so well?
4. What would you do differently next time around?
5. What would you repeat?

Your evaluation process can suit your own needs and style. A round table discussion is sufficient for some groups while others prefer detailed written reports. To be ready to conduct an evaluation, collect information during your marketing effort.

▲ Measure progress on image goals by overall response to the marketing plan; from comments of program participants, board members, funders, and staff; and through interviews with key individuals in the community.

▲ Analyze progress on your action goals by measuring specific results, e.g., percentage increases of participation or contributions, numbers of people attending events.

The data you collect will help you determine what worked, what didn't, and where you might need to improve.

Evaluate Your Marketing Effort

Here is an example of how one program evaluated its marketing success:

The PWI marketing effort—profiled on sample worksheets throughout this book—concludes with a formal report and discussion at a meeting of the program Advisory Board. The report contains the following written information:

All parts of the promotion campaign were carried out as planned.

- Billboards posted: 20
- PSA distribution: all network affiliates, did run on two stations
- Brochures distributed through direct mail: 3,000
- Employers contacted by phone: 200
- In-person sales calls to employers: 75

All goals were met or exceeded:

- The program's new image has clearly taken hold. A review of the most recent month's job postings shows steady demand for janitors and other entry-level positions, but the higher-level jobs are there now, too. Advisory Board members have reported they now talk about PWI differently and realize their own image of the program has changed.
- Job placements remained stable at 250. (Goal: 250)
- Job postings for upper-level positions jumped from 2 to as many as 40 per month. (Goal: 10 per month)
- 30 new employers joined the Employment Committee. (Goal: 20)

The verbal report at the meeting touches on PWI's only marketing problems, which arose, as anticipated, in the production area. First off, the response to the promotion campaign put a tremendous strain on staff. Fitting in all the sales calls and standard follow-up

Continued

wasn't easy. Second, PWI does not always have qualified candidates to respond to the postings that are sent.

Advisory Board members affirm that PWI's image has changed within their own companies and credit the brochure with significant impact. It is then agreed that PWI should deal with its production problem by beefing up its network with other agencies serving people with disabilities to make sure *any* qualified individual in the surrounding area has the opportunity to respond to job openings. It is also agreed that PWI will explore new training programs for its participant population to help prepare people for high-demand occupations of the future.

Neither board nor staff sees the need for a similarly aggressive promotion campaign in the near future, however the campaign brochures will stay in use and all employer contacts will continue to emphasize PWI's new niche as a premier source of qualified applicants for both entry- and management-level jobs.

Evaluation is not just the way to complete a marketing cycle, it is also a beginning. You gain insight and are that much further along in setting goals, lining up the *Ps,* choosing the best promotional techniques, and so on. Marketing requires persistent effort for success. Evaluation helps ensure you persist in the right direction!

▲▲

As your marketing effort takes root, it will build on itself. What initially seemed difficult and overwhelming will later take half the time and produce better results. You will need to be flexible. Through marketing you are opening your doors in a new way and perhaps a bit wider than before. You may be more forthright about what you have to offer, clearer about what you want, and respond more directly to the needs of others.

A marketing challenge that some nonprofits face is being "too far ahead" of their publics. An idea, a service, a commitment, or an art form seems right and important, yet the audience is hard to find or painfully slow to respond.

Steve Jobs, co-founder of Apple Computer and founder of NeXT, Inc., reflects on the "being ahead challenge" in his April 1989 "Entrepreneur of the Decade" interview in **Inc.** magazine.

> I think really great products come from melding two points of view— the technology point of view and the customer point of view. You need both. You can't just ask customers what they want and then try to give that to them. By the time you get it built, they'll want something new... and customers can't anticipate what the technology can do. They won't ask for things that they think are impossible. [5]

Nonprofit creativity produces visions that often run ahead of what others believe is possible. A protected planet. An end to hunger. Loving care for all children. As curators of such visions, the nonprofit marketing task is great. Therein lies the challenge: to light a fire to our promises, to loudly sing their beauty and their value, and to pound the pavement every day until crowds are lined up at our doors.

Nonprofit creativity produces visions that often run ahead of what others believe is possible.

▲▲

[5] Steve Jobs, "Entrepreneur of the Decade, An Interview with Steve Jobs," in **Inc.** (April 1989), p. 114.

Brainstorming

Brainstorming is a way to quickly generate a large number of ideas and involves several ground rules. If working with a group, you will need a leader. That person states specifically what you will be brainstorming about and writes the topic or question at the top of a piece of flip chart paper or on a chalkboard. The leader then encourages the group to brainstorm responses to filling in the blank. For example, if you are working on your organization's image, you might want to brainstorm ways to complete the phrase "We want to be seen as..."

Here are some helpful rules for brainstorming:

▲ Keep the ideas coming; don't stop to analyze or discuss.
▲ There are no "dumb ideas"; don't criticize or edit.
▲ Let go and be creative; anything's OK to say no matter how off the wall.

When brainstorming is finished, have a short discussion to prioritize the "best stuff" that comes out of the exercise.

Visualization

In visualization, people imagine a scene and add in their own dialogue. Here are two possible scenes you might use:

To use visualization for goal-setting, you might imagine you are attending a celebration for your organization in the future, perhaps two or three years from now. The reason for the event is to recognize the wonderful success you have achieved as a result of your marketing effort. The mayor of your city gets up to give a rousing laudatory speech. What is said? What accomplishments are noted?

To use this technique to help get at your positioning statement, imagine you are talking with a person you don't know very well. Perhaps it's someone you meet at a party or a new neighbor. The subject is your work and the other person says, "Oh yes, I've heard of your organization. Now what exactly is it that you do?" You respond, "Oh, we're the people who _____."

Try not to edit your thoughts. Write down the first things that come to mind in the visualization. Later on you can edit them.

Timed writing or drawing

Timed writing or drawing helps you tap into the "stream of consciousness." At the top of a blank piece of paper write the topic on which you want to generate ideas. Check the time, give yourself five minutes, and no matter what the first things are that go on the paper, just start and don't stop until five minutes are up. Some people will want to write, others draw pictures or diagrams, some may do both.

Appendix A

Idea-generating Techniques

You will wind up with lots of material—some embarrassing, some pretty good. If you're working alone, polish up the good stuff and shred the rest. If it's a group activity, ask a few volunteers to interpret their work, discuss where you're heading, and pass everything to a specified writer if you want a final edited piece.

▲▲

The process for answering marketing questions is called *market research*. You can use market research to define the size of a target market, to learn about the attitudes and opinions of your publics, to test a range of assumptions, and much more. The research process can be simple or quite technical and complex.

The most important thing at the outset is to be clear on what questions you want answered. To really benefit from the results, be sure to keep an open mind.

Here are a number of options for how to go about gathering information:

1. Ask around.

It is surely not the most scientific method, but sometimes a few well-placed phone calls or interviews can set you on the right track. You may choose to take what you learn at face value or test the feedback with a wider audience.

2. Look close to home.

If your questions have to do with customer satisfaction, you can learn from the people you already know. Here are suggestions:

▲ Regularly invite your customers or participants to recommend how you can improve.
▲ Follow up with people who show initial interest in your programs or services but don't sign on.
▲ Conduct exit interviews with people who quit programs midway, don't renew season tickets, or in other ways sever their relationship with you.
▲ Look for patterns in why people who apply aren't accepted to your programs.
▲ Ask front-line staff for their observations.

3. Check with known data collectors.

There are plenty of organizations whose job it is to collect and report on all kinds of data. If you're wondering just how many people are out there in any particular category, or how various consumer groups are behaving, you can find out a lot by calling:

▲ United Ways
▲ The Census Bureau
▲ Research centers and institutes
▲ Public libraries
▲ Universities
▲ Research departments of advertising agencies
▲ Many government agencies

Appendix

Market Research

4. Conduct surveys.

Written, telephone, and in-person surveys can tell you a tremendous amount about your publics' opinions and attitudes. For a survey to produce reliable information, however, it must be well designed. ***Do-It-Yourself Marketing Research*** [6] is an accessible and easy-to-follow book for doing just what it says. If you would rather *not* do it yourself, input and assistance are often available at no charge from:

- ▲ Advertising and public relations agencies
- ▲ Business administration graduate students
- ▲ Corporate marketing departments
- ▲ Government agencies

There are also many commercial research firms, some of which specialize in nonprofit areas of concern. Check your Yellow Pages—and references—if you want to consider some paid assistance in designing or carrying out a survey.

5. Hold focus groups.

Although a relatively new type of market research, the popularity of focus groups is growing fast. Focus group research has been credited as a major factor in shaping George Bush's campaign strategy in his successful 1988 bid for the presidency.

Focus group research works like this. A representative sample of a target audience (10–12 people is an ideal group size) is brought together to participate in a discussion usually no longer than one hour. The session produces responses to a pre-determined set of important questions and is facilitated by an outsider or staff member not intimately involved in the subject. The format is carefully structured to elicit straightforward impressions, reactions, and opinions.

The major attraction of focus group research is that it puts you *directly* in touch with your public in a way that allows you to hear the subtleties in their thoughts. You can learn:

- ▲ What people value and why.
- ▲ The specific barriers to "buying" your product.
- ▲ Ideas for changes to remove barriers.
- ▲ What people would do to market your product if they were you.
- ▲ How to speak in the language of your audience (this can sometimes provide exact wording for promotional messages).

The drawbacks to focus group research are the relatively small number of people included and the wholly subjective approach. Focus groups lack the statistical reliability of larger samples. They may tell you quite a bit about what your publics want but reveal nothing about how many members of a particular public are out there to want it.

[6] George Breen and A.B. Blankenship, ***Do-It-Yourself Marketing Research*** (McGraw-Hill, Inc., 1982).

Focus groups are neither time-consuming nor costly. Facilitation of services is quite easily obtained free of charge from students in communications graduate programs or pro bono contributions from ad agencies and corporations. Even when you hire a professional, a modest focus group program is relatively afford-able. Another benefit is the face-to-face relationships that can be established. One nonprofit invited a dozen representatives of rehabilitation agencies to a session on a new home-based employment initiative. Later on, many of the same people became referral sources and some joined a standing advisory committee.

▲

Again, *the most important thing to know about market research is what information you are after.* If you need help deciding what research techniques will be most effective in getting that information—and within your budget and timelines—ask for advice from many of the same resources listed above.

"Side benefits" of market research

Beside providing information you need, there are additional benefits to market research. When you go out into the community and ask questions—especially if you are asking them directly of potential buyers of your product—it is an opportunity to engage people in a positive way and build relationships. Most people enjoy the opportunity to express their opinions and will think well of you for asking. It may also add to their interest or enthusiasm for your product or service.

Tips to maximize the opportunities associated with market research:

1. Be well prepared, gracious, and professional.
2. Make the ultimate findings of the research available to all participants, and follow up on any individual questions or concerns.
3. Provide opportunities, when appropriate, for research participants to be involved further (e.g., consumer advisory councils).
4. Be sure to give research participants the opportunity to buy the product or use the service when it is available.
5. Thank and acknowledge research participants directly and, when warranted, publicly through newsletters, annual reports, announcements to your board and staff, and other types of recognition.

▲▲

Advertising
Great if you can afford it, but not generally considered effective in small quantities. Can work well for special events. Some newspapers and magazines make free space available; most TV and radio stations provide free time. If you *purchase* space or time, ask for nonprofit discounts. Classified ads are a more affordable print advertising option in certain cases. Think about inserting flyers in community newspapers when you want to reach broad audiences.

Annual reports
Considered a "must" by many nonprofits. Be sure to think of this as a promotional tool and apply a marketing approach. Can take the place of an overall brochure, especially if your organization changes a lot year by year. Pay close attention to image, consider innovative approaches, think through distribution.

Atmosphere and Attitude
The first impression you make should reflect your overall standards for quality and service. Think about how your phone is routinely answered. Do people get the feeling you are glad they called? How are people greeted when they walk into your organization? The atmosphere should be pleasant and comfortable, the staff courteous and helpful. Here's a test: if you have a sign at the door, does it say "Welcome!" or "Visitors Must Sign In"?

Billboards
Very affordable through public service programs in many areas. Check with individual companies for rates and availability. Get a good design and use no more than eight words. An excellent way to mix media.

Brochures
Your organizational business card. Not every program needs one—flyers, fact sheets, or other options can do. Think through distribution, pay close attention to image and message, *consider using professionals for copywriting and design,* and remember: many people read only the headlines.

Celebrity Endorsements
Fun and worthwhile, but don't expect too much. This is an attention-getter, but seldom in and of itself "makes the sale."

Direct Mail
Varies widely in effectiveness. If you are considering using this extensively, take a one-day seminar to learn the details. It is really a science. Two tips: 1) It works best once someone already knows who you are and has expressed some interest in you. 2) Good use of mailing lists is essential—testing if you rent or buy them, keeping them updated if you maintain your own.

Direct Sales
Arguably the best promotional technique of all, very labor intensive and most applicable when the "personal touch" is essential. There is a sales truism "People buy from people." If this is part of your plan, here are the essentials: a clear message, good presentation skills, a thorough understanding of the sales process, persistence, and the time to really develop relationships.

Editorials

Newspaper editors are remarkably accessible and will consider well-thought-out, well-documented points of view. Make a phone call first and be prepared to send information right away if you get a positive response. Offers high visibility, is an excellent positioning tool for your organization, and a real contribution to public debate on important issues.

Feature Stories

Reporters are looking for news. If you have something timely, unique, interesting, or new, give it a try. They like a fresh angle, aren't afraid to say no, and may put you off repeatedly for months and then suddenly be on deadline and want to talk to you at 1:00 in the morning. Don't say *anything* you wouldn't want to hear on the news or read in print tomorrow morning. Think through how to take advantage of the maximum effect of feature coverage. Be prepared for high-volume, short-lived response.

Letters to the Editor

When timely, well thought out, and well written, they are very often published. Don't be shy. If you have a strong opinion or your position is being attacked, undermined, or misrepresented by others, get in there and write! Good positioning tool. Your friends and peers will appreciate you for doing this. Like feature coverage, think through how to take advantage of the maximum effect.

Networking

Who you know can mean everything in terms of *access*. Ask board members and friends to introduce you, host meetings, and otherwise convey your message to those you want to hear it. People respond best to initial contacts from people they know.

News Conferences

Only for something very big, very controversial, or very out of the ordinary. If there is anything you can do to make it visually interesting it will help extend coverage. Prepare your message carefully.

News Releases

Can announce anything at all and will often be run if they get to the right person in time. Learn everyone's deadlines and who to address releases to. Check any basic public or media relations textbook for the appropriate professional format. Very good to announce classes, workshops, conferences, special events, and to get in the news if you've won awards, hired management level staff, or otherwise have something newsworthy, but not newsworthy enough to be a feature story. Costs are paper, envelopes, and stamps.

Newsletters

Newsletters let people know you are alive and well and, when well written, can produce loyal readers and good response. Keep them regular. Many people only scan newsletters, so use lots of pictures, headlines, sub-headlines, pull-out quotes, and white space.

Posters

Location is critical. Pay close attention to image. Like billboards, a great way to mix media. A secondary benefit to attractive posters is their staying power. If suitable for framing, they can be around for years.

Public Speaking

Don't just attend conferences, get on the program. Or get out to your local civic clubs, church or synagogue auxiliaries, or any other likely forum. Get coaching or training in order to be a *good* public speaker—all the top professionals do it. Public speaking is a good positioning tool and way to mix media. Have some kind of handout to reinforce your message.

Publishing Articles and Reports

When writing for someone else's publication, be sure you understand its audience and gear the article accordingly. Self-published reports should have crisp executive summaries and appear readable. If you want impact, use a good marketing approach—the influential Washington think tanks do. Excellent positioning tool and sometimes a real opportunity to influence both professional practice and public policy.

Radio Public Service Announcements

Again, check a basic public relations text for professional format. Most stations do not accept tapes—written copy only. Provide 30, 15, and 10 seconds' worth of copy. Expect a two-week lag time before you get on. Excellent way to mix media and costs you nothing but paper, envelopes, and stamps. Thank you notes when you get on the air are a nice touch.

Special Events

Before you do anything else, decide what you want out of the event, then put the elements together accordingly. A good way to renew or maintain personal contacts on a large scale. Remember the invitation itself is a promotional tool. Be careful of special events as fundraising schemes. Expect a sense of let down when it's all over.

Specialty Advertising

A great option when you have a small budget and want to do something fun or unique. Check your Yellow Pages for a company in your area. Someone will be available to show you catalogs with everything from refrigerator magnets to customized mugs to thank you notes with little packages of jelly beans stapled inside. Ask about nonprofit discounts.

Talk Shows

Radio, network, and cable television offer many opportunities for everything from offbeat opinions to live public service announcements to serious discussion. Call and ask to talk to the producer of the show you are interested in. Think through your sales pitch—why this person should have you on their show. If you do get on, write down ahead of time the three things you absolutely want to be sure to say and then, no matter what you are asked, find a way to say them. Depending on the popularity of the show, you can get significant, although short-lived, response. Another great free way to mix media.

Telemarketing

Fancy language for using the phone. Like direct mail, this is a numbers game and something of a science. Look for a one-day seminar to get better educated if you are considering telemarketing on a large scale. Otherwise, think of it as a way to mix media, reinforce relationships, check for quick reactions, and as, well, "the next best thing to being there."

Television Public Service Announcements

Before you go to the trouble of producing a PSA, make sure you know its chances of getting on the air. Every potential broadcaster—including local and national cable—treats them differently. TV stations like PSAs that look like real commercials, so anything you can do to make the grade will help. These can be worth the trouble. TV is a powerful medium and good PSAs have been known to produce excellent response. Local cable stations have many different formats for PSAs. Be sure to check out each one.

Trade Fairs

No one expects to make deals at trade fairs. Your purpose should be to make *contact.* Be sure to have a way to get people's names and addresses. It's the follow-up that can produce the best results. Have a dish of candy at your booth and a take-away item with your name on it that people will be likely to keep and use. (See Specialty Advertising, previous page.)

Videos

When well done and geared to their audience, videos definitely command attention. But what you do with the attention is more important. Look at a video as a part of an overall promotional strategy, never in place of one. It is difficult to get free video production, and costs are steep. In most cases, this is a luxury item.

Word of Mouth

Long called the best kind of advertising, but how do you get it? Three ways. First, by doing what you do *so well* that people are excited and want to talk about it. Second, by making sure everyone associated with your organization is informed, enthusiastic, and pleased to tell anyone and everyone about who you are and what you do. Third, by asking everyone you know to pass along the good word.

1. **Give someone final say.**
   There are many decisions to be made in the process of producing promotional materials. While group input is often valuable, someone has to be able to "sign off" on things and officially declare them ready to go.

2. **You may be a pro bono candidate.**
   Some promotion campaigns are appealing pro bono projects for advertising professionals, especially those on higher profile issues like child abuse, environmental destruction, and AIDS. Pro bono assistance is a great way to get top-notch stuff and stretch your promotion budget. Most free assistance is in the area of creative services and there are often production costs (typesetting, film and processing, printing) attached. Make sure you are aware of the roles, responsibilities, and obligations in a pro bono arrangement and be clear right up front about any special sensitivities you need honored in an advertising campaign.

3. **If it worked in Philadelphia...**
   Many nonprofits have gotten wonderful materials and saved considerable amounts of money by borrowing from other groups in different parts of the country. Reading national journals and being involved in professional networks can produce opportunities of this kind.

4. **Consider hiring professionals.**
   You may have the talent and expertise on staff to produce terrific promotional materials. But if you don't, the services of professional designers and writers can make a real difference. This kind of help can be pricey, but many people will reduce their fees—and at times work for free—for nonprofits. It always pays to ask.

5. **Shop with care.**
   Hire a printer, designer, writer, or mug supplier carefully. It's standard practice for suppliers to make presentations and be interviewed competitively. Look for "good chemistry," how well your specific needs can be met, and ask for bids, as prices can vary widely. If you're not sure where to start, call your local United Way and ask for advice from its communications department.

6. **Take advantage of your suppliers' expertise.**
   You may not be up on the latest design trends, video techniques, or recycled paper stocks, but the suppliers you use will be. Make sure to invite input, ideas, and advice. You can build your own knowledge base and continually add creativity and spark to your promotional tools.

7. **Reduce costs by coordinating production.**
   The more you can think ahead on promotional materials, the greater the possibilities of saving money. There are many economies of scale to be had in design, printing, and purchasing of specialty items. Try to coordinate production of any "families" of promotional materials and look into the advantages of stocking up in advance.

Appendix D

Tips for Implementing Your Promotion Plan

8. **Plan backward from deadlines.**

   When you have a deadline, do your production planning backward from that date. For example, if a brochure on a new program needs to be in people's mailboxes by September 1, allow 10 days for bulk mailing, one week for mail processing, two weeks for printing, three weeks for design and keylines, two weeks for copywriting, one week for content planning, and one week for contingencies. That means you should be starting by June 13. Yes, it can be done faster, but why take chances?

9. **Get training and support.**

   There are many opportunities to build your skill in all aspects of promotion. Excellent one-day training workshops are offered by national as well as local experts. Aside from formal training, look for a promotion mentor. Such a person may work in an advertising or public relations agency, be with a corporation or another nonprofit, or be retired from the field. There is a lot of acquired wisdom in this area and it can be extremely helpful to have someone to turn to for advice.

10. **Enjoy!**

    Promotion can (and should) be fun! It taps your creativity and yields tangible and exciting rewards. You are sure to encounter frustrations, but when success comes along, be sure to celebrate!

▲

If you are producing printed promotional materials yourself, here are additional tips for writing and design.

Writing Tips:

1. **Find examples** of promotional materials you admire and analyze what makes them work for *you.*
2. **Write in language that sells.** It's effective, permitted, and encouraged to violate the rules of good grammar when writing promotional copy. Ads do it all the time. You can even start a sentence with the word, "but" or "and." *Really.*
3. **Use headlines to convey the essentials** of your message and don't forget *the promise of a benefit.*
4. **Keep headlines simple.** That's all there is to say.
5. **Vary sentence length and structure** in your writing. There are many elements to good copy. This is an important one. After you write a rough draft, check it for rhythm and variety. A good way to do this is to read aloud to yourself (close the door first) or collar a friendly listener.
6. In all of what you write, **emphasize benefits** and include information only on the most important features of your product.
7. **Give yourself enough time** so you can finish a draft, put it all aside for a few days, and then give it a fresh look before it's carved in stone.

8. **Show what you write or design to a number of people** and get their reactions and input.
9. **Don't hesitate to do one final edit** to make the copy as short and to the point as possible. Take out the all the "extra" words.

Design Tips:

1. **Keep your eye out for current design trends.** Look at magazines such as ***Print*** and ***Communication Arts*** to see what's being done and get a feel for what you think looks good.
2. **Make sure your design calls attention to what is most important**, is free of "clutter," and helps the copy be as readable as possible.
3. **White space is great.** There is no need to fill up all the space with writing or design. Blank space helps focus the eye on what's important. A page full of copy can look too overwhelming and turn off the reader.
4. **Use clip art.** An unbelievable array of line drawings are available in clip art books and individual sheets. Art supply stores are good places to look.
5. **Don't use too much art** (especially clip art). A little goes a long way in this department. Avoid busy borders and don't stick a picture in a white spot just to fill it.
6. **Use typefaces carefully—and creatively.** Using a variety of styles and sizes helps direct the reader's eye. But don't use too many or too-similar typefaces in one piece. It might look amateurish or like a mistake.
7. **Use accents—with care.** Accents are italics, bolds, boxes, rules, screens, and colors. These are used to highlight certain words or passages. Used sparingly, they do the job. Overused, they lose their punch.
8. **Consider helpful software.** If you are designing on computer there are a number of very specific software packages available. You can get them especially for newsletters, etc.
9. **Step back from your piece for an overall look.** When it's in final draft form, step back and pretend you are looking at it for the very first time. See how all the elements work together.
10. **Go to workshops.** There are excellent workshops on all aspects of promotion—producing newsletters, direct mail, typography, writing copy, etc. Look into local courses at colleges and universities and technical schools as well as seminars presented across the country by a number of professional training firms. Training is sometimes pricey, but often worth it.

▲▲

Bottom-Up Marketing, Al Ries and Jack Trout (McGraw-Hill, Inc., 1989)

The authors' unconventional alternative to traditional marketing planning will spark new ideas.

Cheap But Good Marketing Research, Alan R. Andreasen, (Homewood, IL: Dow Jones-Irwin, 1988)

The facts on concise, accurate, low-cost research—how to make sure every dollar spent yields useful information.

Do-It-Yourself Market Research, George Breen and A.B. Blankenship (McGraw-Hill, Inc., 1982)

Advice for the non-professional marketing researcher on how to run simple, low-cost research studies. Although written for small businesses, nonprofits can use the same techniques to check marketing, service, or product decisions.

Filthy Rich & Other Nonprofit Fantasies: Changing the Way Nonprofits Do Business in the 90's, Dr. Richard Steckel (Berkeley, CA: Ten Speed Press, 1989)

Steckel's unique, common-sense—and irreverent—approach to marketing will help nonprofits explore many new ways to earn money.

The Frugal Marketer: Smart Tips for Stretching Your Budget, J. Donald Weinrauch and Nancy Croft Baker (New York: AMACOM, 1989)

A quick reference tool loaded with innovative marketing tips and ideas. Note especially the sections on marketing research, pricing, sales letters and thanking your customers.

Guide to Public Relations for Nonprofit Organizations and Public Agencies, Or How to Avoid the Potential Perils of Public Relations, Barbara Fultz Martinez and Robert Weiner (Los Angeles: The Grantsmanship Center, 1979)

Excellent short piece on how to deal successfully with all types of media.

In Print: A Concise Guide to Graphic Arts and Printing for Small Businesses and Nonprofit Organizations, Mindy N. Levine with Susan Frank (Englewood Cliffs, NJ: Prentice-Hall, Inc., 1984)

Loads of information on printed pieces—from a simple typewritten press release to a four-color brochure.

Marketing Government and Social Services, John L. Crompton and Charles W. Lamb, Jr. (John Wiley & Sons, Inc., 1986)

A desktop reference guide for public sector executives. Covers all aspects of building an integrated marketing plan for service functions.

Marketing Management: Analysis, Planning, and Control (4th edition), Philip Kotler (Englewood Cliffs, NJ: Prentice-Hall, Inc., 1980)

The essential marketing text by a leading academic expert on marketing.

Appendix
E

Resources

Media in the Public Interest: Talk Radio; Using Video; and ***Cable Access*** (Washington, D.C.: Benton Foundation, 1990)

Three separate booklets discussing under-used communications media and, why, when, and how, nonprofits can use them to their best advantage.

Nonprofit Piggy Goes to Market, Robin Simons, Lisa Farber Miller, and Peter Lengsfelder (Children's Museum of Denver, Inc., 1984)

A light approach to solid, effective marketing practices that worked wonders for the Children's Museum of Denver.

Ogilvy on Advertising, David Ogilvy (New York: Crown Publishers, Inc., 1983)

The essential advertising text by the acknowledged "creative king of the advertising world." His advertising wisdom is as pertinent for nonprofits as it is for Procter & Gamble.

Selling Strategies for Service Businesses: How to Sell What You Can't See, Taste, or Touch, Karen Johnston and Jean Withers (Canada: International Self-Counsel Press Ltd., 1988)

Overcome your distaste for "selling" by learning a comfortable style for nonprofits.

Strategic Media: Designing a Public Interest Campaign (Washington, D.C.: Communications Consortium Media Center, 1990)

A great workbook to encourage nonprofits to think differently—and strategically— about reaching media, and, how to make the media think differently about your organization as a news source.

The Unabashed Self-Promoter's Guide, Dr. Jeffrey Lant (Jeffrey Lant Associates, Inc., 1983)

For the shy person as well as the unabashed, this public relations guide is thorough, practical, and entertaining.

You Are the Message: Secrets of the Master Communicators, Roger Ailes (Homewood, Illinois: Dow Jones Irwin, 1988)

How to be your best when talking with funders, program participants, or the public— or when otherwise marketing your organization.

▲▲

Appendix F

Marketing Worksheets

SECTION A — Action Goals

Complete this worksheet as an individual exercise or include staff and board members. Some people benefit from structured idea-generating techniques such as brainstorming, visualization, and timed writing or drawing to help them set goals. These techniques are described in **Appendix A.**

Instructions
The four steps to setting action goals will help you organize information that should be readily at hand. You may have one or more action goals. Complete the four steps for each of your goals.

1. What are the absolute best results you could hope for? By when?

If you could wave a magic wand, what would appear? (Don't worry if it seems a bit far-fetched. The next steps are designed to bring you down to earth.) If your situation warrants it, try coming up with your ideal for a six-month to three-year period.

Goal: By When:

Goal: By When:

Goal: By When:

2. What outside factors might help or hinder your ability to achieve this ideal?

Goal 1:

Outside factors working **FOR** you: Outside factors working **AGAINST** you:

1.   1.

2.   2.

3.   3.

Continued

SECTION A — Action Goals (continued)

Goal 2:

Outside factors working **FOR** you:

1.

2.

3.

Outside factors working **AGAINST** you:

1.

2.

3.

Goal 3:

Outside factors working **FOR** you:

1.

2.

3.

Outside factors working **AGAINST** you:

1.

2.

3.

Continued

SECTION A — Action Goals (continued)

3. How will realities of budget, staff/volunteer time, and other capabilities affect your effort to achieve these results?

What can you handle? How much in the way of time and resources can you really commit to your marketing effort? Note your answers below:

4. What are your realistic, attainable action goals? By when?

Weigh the ideal results you would like to achieve against the realities of the marketplace and your internal capabilities. Then decide on your goals and the time frame in which you believe you can achieve them.

Goal: By When:

Goal: By When:

Goal: By When:

Continued

SECTION B — Image Goals

1. How are you currently seen by the people or groups most important to you?	2. Are you satisfied with this image?	3. How would you like it to change?
A. People you serve:	A.	A.
B. Others in the community:	B.	B.

*If you aren't sure what your new image should be, the next section in the workbook, **Position Your Organization**, will help you clarify this issue.*

4. How do you want your image to change and with whom? Write your image goal here:

SECTION A — Check in with your mission

1. Write your current mission statement here:

a. Is the mission clear?

b. Does it still provide the right sense of direction for the future?

2. What changes, if any, should be considered in your mission?

SECTION B — Look at needs and how you will address them

For information to complete this section, turn first to your clients and staff. They're the best sources you have. However, sometimes staff and clients are too close to issues and current programs to see what changes in focus could produce even greater impact. Add some outside perspective, too.

1. List the most critical ongoing or emerging community needs you will address.

2. Outline ideas for how you might respond.

Continued

SECTION C — Survey the competition to see how you fit in

1. Who are your competitors ?

2. What are you competing for?

3. How do your outstanding strengths compare with theirs?

4. List potential partners and how you might team up with each.

Continued

There are four general ways competition affects decisions on positioning. After surveying the competition, how do things look for you? Check all those that apply:

☐ There are needs to be met and we're exactly the people to do the job.

☐ It will be best to meet needs through a collaborative venture.

☐ Needs we identified are being met to some degree, but our contribution is necessary and unique, so we'll compete.

☐ The needs we identified are being met very well by others; we should back off.

SECTION D — Draft your positioning statement

Your positioning statement should make it easy for people to quickly grasp who you are and what unique role you want to play.

1. **To develop material for your statement, first complete the following phrases in as many ways as you can think of. (Instructions for three structured ways to generate ideas is provided in Appendix A.)**

   a. We're the people who...

   b. No one but no one can _____ as well as we do.

   c. We want to be seen as...

2. **Now go back and circle the phrases that most strongly convey who you are and what unique role you want to play.**

Continued

3. Based on the circled phrases in Section D, and applying the four criteria for positioning statements *(short and to the point, uses everyday language, conveys character, and has a sense of action)*, write your draft statement here:

SECTION E — Test your positioning statement for support

1. List at least three key potential sources of support with whom you will test your positioning statement.

2. Make appointments with these people or groups and, in each case, gain answers to these four questions:

   a. Based on your knowledge of our organization and this community, do you agree this is how we should be positioned?

   b. Why or why not?

   c. How might we modify our ideas to improve them?

   d. Are there other people or groups you would recommend we talk with?

SECTION F — Refine and clarify your positioning statement

Write your revised positioning statement here:

SECTION A — Product—What you offer

1. What is the product?

2. Is there anything about your product that makes it difficult to understand or use?

✔ *Product Checkpoint*—Is your product in line? Is it of high quality and does it meet a specific need?

☐ OK   ☐ Need information   ☐ Adjustment necessary   ☐ Feature to promote

Write your questions, adjustments needed, and promotion notes on Worksheet 4.

SECTION B — Publics—Those with whom you want to make exchanges

1. Make a complete list of your publics for each major product or program.

Continued

SECTION B — Publics (continued)

2. Choose your primary publics for each product and note the benefits of the product they value most.

Primary Publics	Benefits

✔ *Publics Checkpoint*—Are your publics in line? Do you have the "right" publics and know what benefits you provide?

☐ OK ☐ Need information ☐ Adjustment necessary ☐ Feature to promote

Write your questions, adjustments needed, and promotion notes on Worksheet 4.

SECTION C — Price—How much you charge

1. What are you asking for? Dollars and cents or something else?

2. How much do you charge?

3. Could your customers—or at least some of them—pay more?

✔ *Price Checkpoint*—Is your price in line? Not too high, not too low?

☐ OK ☐ Need information ☐ Adjustment necessary ☐ Feature to promote

Write your questions, adjustments needed, and promotion notes on Worksheet 4.

Continued

SECTION D — Place—Where the product is available

1. Do people come to you or do you bring your product to them?

2. Are there any place "barriers" you should address?

✔ *Place Checkpoint*—Is place in line? Are you accessible to your publics?

☐ OK ☐ Need information ☐ Adjustment necessary ☐ Feature to promote

Write your questions, adjustments needed, and promotion notes on Worksheet 4.

SECTION E — Production—The ability to meet demand

1. Can you effectively meet demand?

2. What if demand increases—or falls?

✔ *Production Checkpoint*—Is production in line? Can you effectively meet demand?

☐ OK ☐ Need information ☐ Adjustment necessary ☐ Feature to promote

Write your questions, adjustments needed, and promotion notes on Worksheet 4.

Continued

SECTION F — Promotion—What you do to motivate people to respond

1. What promotional techniques have you used? (See Appendix C for annotated list of techniques.) Note the effectiveness of each by placing a check in the appropriate column and add any comments you have.

Technique	Effective	Not effective	Not sure	Comments

✔ *Promotion Checkpoint*—Is promotion in line? Do you use effective techniques that motivate people to respond?

☐ OK   ☐ Need information   ☐ Adjustment necessary

Write your questions, adjustments needed, and promotion notes on Worksheet 4.

SECTION A — Information needed

If you checked *need information* in any of the sections on Worksheet 3, write the specific questions you want answers to below:

1.

2.

3.

4.

5.

6.

7.

8.

9.

10.

Continued

SECTION B — Adjustments necessary

If you checked *adjustment necessary* in any of the sections on Worksheet 3, note the specific problems needing attention below:

1.

2.

3.

4.

5.

6.

7.

8.

9.

10.

Continued

SECTION C — Promotion notes

If you checked *feature to promote* in any of the sections on Worksheet 3 or have other ideas on promotion that come up during the audit, elaborate below:

1.

2.

3.

4.

5.

6.

7.

8.

9.

10.

SECTION A — Marketing goals

Write your marketing goals here:

SECTION B — The plan

1. The product is: Comments:

2. It will be marketed to these primary publics who value particular benefits of the product:

Primary Publics   Benefit   Comments:

Continued

SECTION B — The plan (continued)

3. **At this price:**   **Comments:**

4. **Available at this (these) location(s):**   **Comments:**

5. **To effectively meet demand we will:**   **Comments:**

6. **The major features to promote are:**   **Comments:**

   Our basic approach to promotion will include: **Comments:**

Continued

SECTION C — Implementation

Step	Responsibility	Deadline	Budget

SECTION A — Image

An effective image says what you'd like it to say, captures your uniqueness, and stands out in a crowd.

1. **Write a list of colorful and descriptive words or phrases that best describe how you would like your organization to be seen:**

2. **Circle the above items that do the best job of describing the image you would like for your organization or product.**

SECTION B — Message

An effective message motivates your audience to take a specific action and promises a desirable benefit if they do.

1. **In two or three sentences, describe the average person for whom your message is intended. What are their special circumstances and sensitivities?**

Continued

SECTION B — Message (continued)

2. What barriers or resistance to your promotional message might you have to meet and overcome?

3. What specific action do you want people to take as a result of your message?

4. In order of importance to your target audience, what are the top three benefits and features you offer?

5. What is your message?

Continued

SECTION C — Techniques

The principles for an effective combination are: 1) Gear tools to the audience 2) Plan how each can be used to maximum effect 3) Pick the right mix—within budget 4) Frequency over time equals reach 5) If it worked, do it again 6) Don't abandon the basics 7) Stay the course. Make the choices you believe will be most effective, keeping in mind budget constraints and how much effort you can realistically put into development and follow-through.

1. Check the techniques that you would like to combine in a promotion campaign.

☐ Advertising   ☐ Newsletters
☐ Annual reports   ☐ Posters
☐ Attitude and Atmosphere   ☐ Public Speaking
☐ Billboards   ☐ Publishing Articles and Reports
☐ Brochures   ☐ Radio Public Service Announcements
☐ Celebrity Endorsements   ☐ Special Events
☐ Direct Mail   ☐ Specialty Advertising
☐ Direct Sales   ☐ Talk Shows
☐ Editorials   ☐ Telemarketing
☐ Feature Stories   ☐ Television Public Service Announcements
☐ Letters to the Editor   ☐ Trade Fairs
☐ Networking   ☐ Videos
☐ News Conferences   ☐ Word of Mouth
☐ News Releases

2. How will these techniques work together to produce the response you want?

Continued

SECTION D — Implementation

Step	Responsibility	Deadline	Budget